Dick Tiger

The Life & Times of Africa's
Most Accomplished World Boxing
Champion
New Edition

'DAMOLA IFATUROTI

AMVPS

Published by
AMV Publishing Services
259 Nassau Street Ste 2 #661
Princeton NJ 08542-4609
Tel: + 1 609-627-9168 - Fax: + 1 609-716-7224
emails: publisher@amvpublishingservices.com &
customerservice@amvpublishingservices.com
worldwide web: https://amvpublishingservices.com

Dick Tiger The Life and Times of Africa's Most Accomplished World Boxing Champion New Edition

Copyright © 2023 'Damola Ifaturoti
First published in the USA in 2002 by
Sungai Corp.
P.O. Box 3295
Princeton, NJ 08543-3295

All rights reserved. No part of this publication may be reproduced, stored in a retrieval system, or transmitted in any form or by any means, electronic, mechanical, photocopying, recording or otherwise without the written permission of the Publisher.

Book & Cover Design: AMV Origination & Design Division

Library of Congress Control Number: 2022944678

ISBN: 978-099-847-969-9

Contents

Dedication v

Foreword to the Second Edition vi

Original Acknowledgments ix

Original Foreword by Chief Achike Udenwa Executive Governor, Imo State of Nigeria, 2002 xvi

Prologue: Dick Tiger in Historical Perspective xx

Chronological Highlights of Dick Tiger's Life and Boxing Career xxv

Chart 1: The Professional Fight Record of Dick Tiger xxix

Chapter One: Origins and Early Professional Career 1

Chapter Two: Liverpool: Fighter in a Strange Land 7

Chapter Three: Tiger in America 13

Chapter Four: Enter the Tiger: The First World Championship Reign 19

Photographs...25

Chapter Five: The Multiple Champion and the Nigerian Civil War 63

Chapter Six: A Full Circle 77

Epilogue: The Legacy of Africa's Most Accomplished Boxer 83

Afterword..90

Appendix 1: Author's article "25 Years After his Death Dick Tiger Remains a Champion" published in *The Ring* Magazine January 1997 issue 92

Appendix 2: Book Review Published in *The Ring* Magazine, July 2002 97

Appendix 3: Author's article "The Best of a Nation: The All Time Top Ten of Africa" published in *The Ring* Magazine April 1996 issue......98

Bibliography 100

About the Author......102

Index 105

Dedication

A wise saying of the Igbo ethnic group of Nigeria, from among whom the subject of this biography, Richard Ihetu a.k.a. Dick Tiger was born, is that *A Man's deeds are his Life.* Another Nigerian ethnic adage posits that *One must row in whichever boat one finds oneself.*

These two proverbs, the first on self-actualization and the other on loyalty and perseverance, may be said to reflect the virtues, which were the hallmarks of the subject's life as will be shown in this simple account of his life.

This biography is dedicated to none other than the subject himself. In writing his life story, my goal is three-fold: to rekindle the world's memory of the great African boxer; to rehabilitate his image; and to acknowledge his virtuous legacy as a truly selfless individual who sacrificed much in the interest of his kinsmen.

Foreword to the Second Edition

It has been two decades since the original edition of this biography, *Dick Tiger: The Life & Times of Africa's Most Accomplished World Boxing Champion* was published in the US. At public presentations of the book in New York and Atlanta in 2002, I stressed my two main goals for writing the biography, the first being to highlight the great African boxer to the world at large and the second to chronicle for posterity, his still unsurpassed professional record and thereby acknowledge his great legacy as a fighter. While I cannot, in all honesty, claim that the book has fully achieved these goals in the years since its original publication, the responses I received personally from far flung places around the globe, nonetheless were quite positive as to provide me with a sense of quiet satisfaction and indeed vindication of my labor of love in writing the biography.

Largely through the good offices of *The Ring* Magazine's erstwhile Editor-in-Chief, Nigel Collins who kindly attended the book presentation in New York, held at the Nigerian Consulate in Manhattan in early 2002 and then published a review of the biography in the July 2002 edition of "The Bible of Boxing," (see Appendix 2 on page 97), I received a steady flow of correspondence, information requests and orders from both individuals and corporate bodies in cities across the US, Canada, England, Scotland, South Africa, Tanzania, Australia and New Zealand.

Foreword to the Second Edition

The encouraging public response from the different countries highlighted has spurred me into this effort of having a new edition of the biography published under a new imprint. The new edition is an attempt at improving both the presentation and packaging of the earlier edition and also making an e-book version available for the ever growing reading audience that relies on electronic readers. The new edition contains substantially much of the earlier information and data in the first, with particular attention placed on rectifying the few minor typographical errors that had earlier escaped detection and updating particular details where necessary. The goals remain the same and it is hoped that in addition to a continuation of the favorable responses from the international reading audience, a much improved feedback from the local Nigerian readership will also be achieved. There is no gainsaying that old adage that *charity begins at home* and so it should be for Dick Tiger, whose great professional and personal achievements should be rightly appreciated by his own fellow country men and women wherever they come from within the Nigerian federation. Only under this light can the subject truly be seen as a credit to his homeland by the international community.

Finally, in this foreword to the new edition, I again express my gratitude to the various individuals, institutions and corporate bodies that supported my original efforts to write the biography in the first place, as noted in the acknowledgments of the first edition. Additionally, however, I would also like to thank a variety of other individuals and groups who have since then, provided positive feedback and sent me kind words of commendation for the biography. At the expense of sacrificing brevity, but with no regrets whatsoever for this, I detail below an alphabetical list of all these particular benefactors, to whom

I owe a great debt of gratitude: Jide Adedeji, Sam Adepegba, Dolapo Akinwande, Chii Akporji, Ganiu Alabi, John Barbella, Shawn Barber, Christopher J. Baubel, Samuel W. Bearman, Ernest D. Brown, James A. Brown, Jeff Brown, Walter Cummings, J. Karel de Vries (South Africa), Gboyega Delano, John Di Arenzo, Robert Dunn, William Ebhomielen, now late Oladunjoye Esan, Toyin Falola, Robert Fanelli, Segun Fayemi, David Hall, Bill Hughes (Scotland), Muyiwa Idowu, David Joseph, Pat Kennedy, now late Soji Lagunju, Richard Lucero, Matt Mankelow (Sportspages UK), Billy Martinez, Norman Montgomery, Kent C. Motsinger, Clay Moyle, Abdul-Rasheed Na'Allah, Kevin R. Oliver, J. Newbold (New Zealand), John Nolan, Nmutaka Okongwu, Ola Opaleye, Greg Pier, Maureen Sacks (Peltz Boxing Promtions, Inc.), Louis D. Scalzetto, Gregory Scott, Aissata G. Sidikou, Abdu Simba (Tanzania), Lekan Soyemi, Neil V. Terens, and James K. White.

'Damola Ifaturoti
Princeton Junction, New Jersey
September 2022

Original Acknowledgments

When I embarked upon this biographical project, I anticipated that writing the life story of a subject who had been dead for over a quarter-century would be a daunting one. Clearly, the passage of such a lengthy period was bound to place severe handicaps on my efforts to assemble accurately, all the important details and events of the subject's life. Likewise, I expected that the task of verifying and authenticating facts and figures would be a difficult one. However, once I commenced the exercise, I discovered that these handicaps were further compounded by the reality that many of the official records on the subject had been lost to, or obscured by the vicissitudes of Nigeria's civil war between 1967 and 1970.

It is therefore pertinent that I note from the onset that this biographical project on Richard Ihetu a.k.a. Dick Tiger was fraught with all sorts of constraints, which I was only able to overcome due to the goodwill and support of various individuals, institutions, and bodies. I am greatly indebted to these varied benefactors and acknowledge that bringing the project to fruition could not have been possible without them all. To all these groups and individuals, I am duty bound to express my gratitude.

To start with, I must thank *The Ring* Magazine for indirectly providing me with the *raison d'être* for embarking on the project in the first place. My primary motivation to write the life story of Dick Tiger followed the publication of a twenty-fifth anniversary tribute I had written on him for *The Ring*, as a freelance writer in late 1996, which was published in the magazine's January 1997 issue (see Appendix 1 on page 92). While preparing the tribute, I had been astonished not to find any full-length biography of the subject, despite his remarkable professional achievements in boxing at both national and international levels. I thus resolved to rectify what I considered a glaring omission from the available literature on Africa's modern sports heroes by privately researching into the life and times of the subject and working to have my findings published into a full-length biography for both national and international reading audiences.

In the course of my research on the biography in mid-1998, I visited *The Ring*'s headquarters in Ambler, Pennsylvania. The magazine's editor-in-chief, Nigel Collins and (now erstwhile) vice president (marketing), David M. Gerhadt received me very warmly and both showed keen interest in my proposed biography. They kindly allowed me access to information and data from the extensive archives of *The Ring* as well as material from the vast photo-library of the magazine.

Aside the moral and material support these two fine gentlemen provided me on behalf of their boxing journal, each was also a source of personal encouragement and inspiration for me on the project. Indeed, I learnt first-hand from my trip to Ambler why Nat Fleischer and his co-founders of *The Ring* chose for the magazine that seemingly sacrilegious subtitle *"The Bible of Boxing"* at the founding of the magazine in 1922. It clearly was not for mere rhetoric or a promotional hyperbole. The dedication with which *The Ring* has taken on its role of documentation and

Original Acknowledgments

projection of the sport's development over the years has been nothing short of religious. I wish *The Ring* continued success and many more years of providing boxing fans the world over with quality reporting and analyses on the sport.

My gratitude also goes to the World Boxing Association (WBA) for the support the body provided me by way of verification of facts, statistics and other relevant data. I thank WBA President Gilberto DeJesus Mendoza and the executive director of the association's central office, Gilberto Mendoza Jr., who both responded positively to my solicitations for information when I contacted them at their headquarters in Venezuela. No doubt, the cooperation of these helmsmen of the WBA was freely given to me in their conviction that the life of Dick Tiger, one of the WBA's first African born world champions, was a worthy one that deserved to be chronicled for posterity. Thanks again, Messrs. Mendoza and Mendoza, Jr.

I am also greatly indebted to a number of contacts that assisted me during my research at home in Nigeria. I thank Toyin Akinoso, to whom I was introduced in Lagos by my good friends, Seye Fadahunsi and Lanre Omisore. Toyin turned out an invaluable contact in Nigeria's journalistic circles, providing me with very useful references to among others, Dr. Onukaba Adinoyi-Ojo, managing director of Nigeria's oldest daily newspaper, *The Daily Times*. With the assistance of Dr. Adinoyi-Ojo, I was able to procure from *The Times'* photo library, several interesting and rare photographs of the subject, his wife and children, which no doubt add to the overall appeal of this biography. Mention must also be made of my gratitude and thanks to some other good old friends for their goodwill and support. My thanks to Seun Mabogunje who had earlier on provided me the assistance of a personal aide of his in ferreting for information regarding the whereabouts of an old contact in the Nigerian press. I also thank two good friends based in New York; Sola Oyebolu and Dayo Owotomo for their material and moral support. Thanks too, to my dear brother, Fela Ifaturoti who provided me with one of my first sources of researching the subject matter via the INTERNET from his base in Kent, England. Thanks also to my dear longstanding family friend and benefactor in more ways than one, Oye Ajayi-Obe, who took me around in the Bronx and Manhattan on a number of my research missions to New York City.

All in all, at home and abroad I solicited comments and opinions regarding varied aspects of the subject's life from several individuals connected with boxing in various capacities. A number of long standing followers of the fight game were consulted for their insights and knowledge on the sport as well as the subject's professional record and personal life. I have also quoted from articles of various writers in newspapers, journals and magazines, some dating as far back as the late 1950s. These varied sources include Tiger's fellow boxers and former world champions, fight officials, boxing historians, record keepers, sports journalists etc. To each and every one of them, I convey my special thanks and gratitude. For the sake of brevity, I can mention only a few here directly by name; Chief Ganiyu Kolawole Balogun, Ralph Citro, Steve Farhood, Gene Fullmer, Lloyd Garrison, Joey Giardello, and Phil Pepe. A short bibliography of books, journals, magazines and web sites is presented at the conclusion of this brief biography in acknowledgement of writers whose earlier works have aided me on the project.

Original Acknowledgments

Before concluding my acknowledgments however, I would be remiss if I do not note the support and understanding of the "home front". Indeed, the time and effort put into researching into and chronicling the life of a "long forgotten" sporting hero was at the cost of sacrificing considerable time and energy for family matters. I thank my dear partner and loving wife, Lola and our four children, Olamide (Toni), Oyinade, Ayotunde and Semilore for putting up with my diversions away from household and family duties during the months of my researching and writing. This expression of gratitude is all the more essential considering that this project started at a time when we had all just recently relocated from Nigeria to the United States and we were still undergoing the throes of having to readjust our lives and settle into a new environment in Indiana. While on the home front, I am also duty-bound to acknowledge the great support I have received over the years from my dear parents, the late Loja Michael Adebayo Ifaturoti (1925-2007) and Mrs. Olusolape Ifaturoti and siblings, Sade, Fela, Yemi and Tolu, who have always encouraged me in all my endeavors.

Here, I must also thank Sungai Books for accepting to publish this biography. A number of other publishing houses had earlier turned down the manuscript, or offered very unfavorable publishing contracts, not wishing to risk investing in a book project that they perceived as not having an assured commercial appeal and marketability. I believe the Publisher, Dr. Ugorji Ugorji seized the gauntlet which others had run shy off, and accepted to publish this biography in recognition of the contribution, no matter how humble, which the work makes to the sporting and general history of the Nigerian nation, her diverse peoples and Africa in general. In his conviction of the significance of the biography, the Publisher went the extra mile of inviting the incumbent governor of the late subject's home state in Nigeria, Chief Achike Udenwa to write a foreword, which the governor so graciously accepted. I cannot thank Chief Udenwa enough for pitting his official weight behind this biography and I am deeply honored and humbled by his kind endorsement of the work.

In conclusion, of all the good people that facilitated the fulfillment of my goal of writing this biography, none could be as important or more relevant to the subject matter than the Ihetu family themselves. Finally in June 2001, nearly four years after commencing the project, I was able to make contact with one of the subject's four daughters, Ms. Justina Ihetu who lives in New York City with her family. This was made possible by the publisher, Dr. Ugorji, who happened to have met Justina a number of years back, without having known of her blood ties to the champion. Following his acceptance to publish the biography, Ugorji made efforts to trace the family and only then learnt that Justina was one of the subject's daughters. He reestablished contact and informed her of the project on her father's life, while sending her a copy of the draft manuscript and inquiring if she would be willing to meet with me. Following his prompting, I contacted Justina and after cautious consideration, she kindly agreed to grant me audience in her home in the Bronx for an interview with her mother. Apparently, Mrs. Abigail Ihetu, Tiger's widow and matriarch of the family, was soon arriving from Nigeria to visit with Justina and her other siblings based in the United States. The meeting eventually took place on Sunday August 26, 2001, and I cannot adequately convey the depth of my gratitude and respect to

Original Acknowledgments

Mrs. Ihetu and Justina for sharing cherished memories of their dearly departed husband and father with me. Indeed, from talking to them I was able to clarify a number of controversial and salient issues on the personal life of the subject and the biography has been made more accurate by this contact.

Finally, and most importantly I give thanks to The One, who makes all things possible, God The Creator, for giving me the will and the ability to see the project through and for enabling the work to see the light of day.

'Damola Ifaturoti
Plainsboro, New Jersey,
September, 2001

Original Foreword

By Chief Achike Udenwa,
Executive Governor of Imo State, 2002

When a man as proud as this wants to fight, he does not care if his own head rolls as well in the conflict.
                                    Chinua Achebe in *Arrow of God.*

Few Nigerians have transcended the nation's boundaries to become world figures. The late Richard Ihetu (also known as Dick Tiger) was much more than an African icon, he was a world champion in more ways than one. His legacy was left not only on the canvass of boxing, but more importantly in the hearts of the kinsmen for whom he sacrificed a lot.

I am delighted to write the Foreword to this biography. Dick Tiger was from the great state of Imo, where I have the honor and humility in serving as the current chief executive. So, with gratitude to both the author, Mr. 'Damola Ifaturoti, and the publisher, Dr. Ugorji O. Ugorji, I offer these few words on behalf of all people who saw in Dick Tiger, images of greatness both in sports and in humanity.

During the brief 42 years of his remarkable life, this son of a chicken farmer from Amaigbo Orlu, appeared like a shooting star and took his place in the galaxy of human history. In

Original Foreword

doing so, he made history as the first African born pugilist to win undisputed world boxing championships in two different classes. He would become world champion three times, securing for himself, as Ifaturoti asserts, the status of Africa's most accomplished world boxing champion in modern history.

In many ways the Dick Tiger story is the story of his kinsmen. From the obscurity of the commercial city of Aba, and through hard work, fortified with a quintessential sense of purpose, he rose to command the respect of the world. As is characteristic of his kinsmen, he traveled the world over, making every port of call a home away from home. And when fate called for men to come home and stand up for what was right, as it did from 1967 to 1970 in Nigeria, he risked everything and chose his kinsmen over the accolades of opportunism. Nigeria, the nation whose flags he carried proudly into the rings as world champion, has never given this legend the recognition and celebration he deserves. Ifaturoti is doing so in *Dick Tiger: The Life and Times of Africa's Most Accomplished World Boxing Champion.*

It is particularly remarkable that this biographical effort has been put together, not by one of Dick Tiger's kinsmen, but by our brother from the Western axis of the River Niger divide. Ifaturoti must be praised and celebrated for this effort. Besides the exciting and authoritative information that the book offers readers, *Dick Tiger: The Life and Times of Africa's Most Accomplished World Boxing Champion* is a timely and welcome contribution in Nigeria's on-going soul search for our purpose as a nation, and for a more perfect federation.

The reality of boxing, nonetheless, is that it remains the preserve of poor young men. It is rare that a well educated child from a background of opulence makes boxing a career choice. And while all sports, including boxing, must be encouraged and celebrated in Nigeria, those of us in government must ensure that every child gets the kind of education and employment opportunities where the choice of boxing or any other sport, as a career, is out of love and gift for the sport, not as a matter of simple survival.

We in Imo State have been blessed over the years with the gift of the brightest and most hard working students in Nigeria. Unfortunately, the education of our youth in environments that are comfortable enough to facilitate learning, had been neglected by past (military) administrations. My administration has made tremendous strides in our declared mission to reverse that legacy. We still have a long way to go, but I am irrevocably committed to providing, within the confines of our limited resources, the type of quality education (including well trained and well compensated teachers) that our students and scholars deserve.

I must commend the publisher of Sungai Books for his commitment in facilitating the revitalization of the educational enterprise in Nigeria.

Sungai Books has become the audacious outlet for such works as *Dick Tiger: The Life and Times of Africa's Most Accomplished World Boxing Champion*. I look forward to the completion of its African headquarters at Owerri.

I highly recommend the book. As a piece of literature, the unlabored writing style makes the book quite easy to read

Original Foreword

and comprehend. In this document of recorded history, the author educates and enlightens superlatively, and succeeds in reminding us of our capacity for greatness, both individually (in the case of Richard Ihetu), and collectively as a nation.

May the glorious and triumphant spirit of Dick Tiger continue to inspire us all.

Chief Achike Udenwa
Executive Governor,
Imo State Government House,
Owerri 2002

Prologue

Dick Tiger in Historical Perspective

After over half a century since his passing on December 14, 1971, the records show that Dick Tiger still remains Africa's most internationally accomplished boxer in the modern era of the sport. He was Africa's first multiple world champion, and a three-time undisputed titleholder in two of the sport's traditional eight weight divisions. This is a feat yet to be equaled by any other African boxer to date.

Tiger twice held the undisputed world middleweight championship. He initially won the National Boxing Association (NBA) version of the title on October 23, 1962 by defeating Gene Fullmer in San Francisco, California USA. The following year, the Nigerian born boxer secured undisputed recognition after defeating Fullmer in their third bout fought in Ibadan, Nigeria. Tiger lost the title to Joey Giardello on December 7, 1963 when he was defeated by the American challenger at the Madison Square Garden, New York City, by a close 15-round decision.

Two years later on October 21, 1965, Tiger regained the title from Giardello. He held on to the laurel for another six months, giving it up via a 15-round points loss to Emile Griffith of the Virgin Islands on April 25, of 1966.

Prologue: Dick Tiger in Historical Perspective

On December 16, 1966, in his very next fight, Tiger won the undisputed world light heavyweight title from Puerto Rico's Jose Torres. In the entire history of the modern era of Boxing, only one other fighter, British born Bob Fitzsimmons, had up till this time, won both the world's middleweight and light heavyweight championships. Tiger held the 175-pound crown for nearly a year and a half before being dethroned by America's Bob Foster on May 24, 1968.

To date, no other African boxer has been able to match Tiger's achievement of having won both the undisputed world middleweight and light heavyweight titles, not to talk of surpassing it. This has been in spite of an unhealthy development in the sport in recent years—the gross proliferation of governing bodies and weight divisions—that has resulted in a ludicrous multiplicity (and oftentimes duplication) of "world" titles and "world" titleholders.

Tiger fought at a time when there was more unity, cohesion and order in the governing of boxing. Aside from the New York State Athletic Commission (NYAC), which was basically an American organization, there was only one major world governing body, the National Boxing Association (NBA) which later metamorphosed into the World Boxing Association (WBA). At the time, there were eight traditional weight divisions comprising flyweight (limit: 112 pounds), bantamweight (limit 118 pounds), featherweight (limit 126 pounds), lightweight (limit 135 pounds), welterweight (limit 147 pounds), middleweight (limit 160 pounds), light Heavyweight (limit 175 pounds) and heavyweight (over 175 pounds).

Today boxing is saddled with a superfluity of controlling organizations and sanctioning bodies each with its own exclusive "world champions". In addition, there are at least 18 weight classes with several so-called junior divisions having been created in more recent times. This has led to a carnival-like scenario for boxing as a sport, wherein titles have become a dime a dozen and there are rarely any truly undisputed world champions any more. Had Tiger fought in the present times, it is likely he would have easily won titles in at least two additional weight classes i.e., the junior middleweight and super middleweight divisions. However, the reader should not misconstrue this writer as belittling the accomplishments of African boxers that have followed Tiger or even those that came before him. Indeed, over the years, a number of African boxers have also excelled in their respective divisions and thus deserve the respect that is due to true world champions that they were. These fine African-born champions are worthy of mention here in properly placing Tiger's achievements among his peers in historical perspective. See Appendix 3 on page 98 providing the author's article "The All Time Top 10 of Africa (Excluding South Africa)" written for *The Ring* Magazine in 1996.

Probably the most notable of African boxers of contemporary times is the Ghanaian, Azumah Nelson, whose professional fight career was from 1979 to 2008. Nelson won world titles at two weight classes i.e., featherweight, 1984-1988, and twice at super featherweight, 1988-1994, and 1995-1997 under the aegis of the World Boxing Council. The hardy Ghanaian enjoyed lengthy reigns in both divisions. However, "The Professor", as Nelson was affectionately nicknamed by the boxing fraternity, was never an undisputed world champion. Also having won titles at weight divisions considerably lower than Tiger's, it

Prologue: Dick Tiger in Historical Perspective

may be argued further, that the Ghanaian's achievements fell short of the Nigerian's.

Amadou Louis M'Barick Fall (Battling Siki) of Senegal is also worthy of mention here among outstanding African pugilists during the modern era of the sport. Overcoming great odds, Siki dethroned world light heavyweight champion and popular French idol, Georges Carpentier in Paris on September 24, 1922, thereby becoming the first African-born World champion in modern boxing history. However, Siki's ephemeral reign of barely six months and the subsequent multiple losses he suffered in the ring, preclude him from serious contention as Africa's greatest fighter though his historical significance as the first African world champion can never be denied him. Another outstanding African pugilist of contemporary times that preceded Tiger was Nigeria's Hogan "Kid" Bassey, undisputed World Featherweight Champion between 1957 and 1959, who died on January 26, 1998, at age 66. Ayub Kalule of Uganda, WBA junior middleweight title from 1979 to 1982, and the Italy-based Zairean, Sumbu Kalambay, WBA middleweight titleholder from 1987 to 1988, also fit into the pantheon of worthy African born world champions.

Also not to be overlooked from the list of the finest fighters from Africa are two Ugandans: Cornelius Boza-Edwards, WBC junior lightweight champion in 1981, and John "The Beast" Mugabi, WBC junior middleweight titlist from 1989 to 1990. Two other Ghanaians complete this roll call of great African fighters: David Kotey, WBC world featherweight title holder from 1975 to 1976, and Ike Quartey, WBA welterweight champion from 1994 to 1998. None of these fine champions however, can match Dick Tiger's multiple world championship record or the international acclaim the Nigerian won at the peak of his boxing career.

However, Tiger's appeal as a biographical subject transcends his achievements in Boxing's vicious square ring alone. It will be shown in this concise account of his life that despite the fact that his destiny was shaped by the vicissitudes of a bloody war between Nigeria and the breakaway Biafra, Tiger was the very epitome of gentility, selflessness and humility. Indeed, a more honorable and complete gentleman can hardly be found in the annals of the usually chaotic sport of fist fighting.

This brief biography seeks to bring to light the hitherto largely neglected great legacy of Dick Tiger, not only for a new generation of his Nigerian countrymen and fellow Africans but indeed also for the whole world at large. By recalling the events of his noble life and highlighting his sterling professional accomplishments, it is hoped that Dick Tiger will finally be fully appreciated and acknowledged for what he was— A truly great African sports hero—and a man of conscience and valor who deserves to be accorded the respect and honor of a great hero.

Chronological Highlights of Dick Tiger's Life and Boxing Career

August 14 1929 — Dick Tiger is born Richard Ihetu in Amaigbo. The small rural village was at the time situated in the Eastern Region of the British West African colonial territory of Nigeria. Following the adoption of a federal system of government and the creation of states after independence, Amaigbo Orlu is now in the Imo State of Nigeria.

1952 — Dick Tiger began boxing professionally in Nigeria at the age of 23.

1953/1954 — Contested twice for the Nigerian national middleweight title in Lagos, Nigeria.

December, 1955 — moved to Liverpool, England to continue campaigning professionally as a boxer in the U.K.

March, 1958 — won vacant British Empire (Commonwealth) middleweight title in Liverpool, England by defeating Pat McAteer.

1959 — following his marriage to Abigail (nee Ogbuji), Dick Tiger moved to the USA to further enhance his pursuit of international laurels in professional boxing.

1960 — lost and regained the British Empire (Commonwealth) middleweight title from Wilf Greaves in Alberta, Canada.

DICK TIGER

1961 — gained recognition as the number one contender for the world middleweight championship title.

1962 — won the National Boxing Association (NBA) world middleweight title from Gene Fullmer in San Francisco California, USA.

1962 — Dick Tiger is honored as "Fighter of the Year" by both *The Ring* Magazine and the Boxing Writers Association of America (BWAA).

August, 1963 — won recognition as undisputed world middleweight champion following rematch against Gene Fullmer in Ibadan, Nigeria.

1963 — Dick Tiger is honored with membership into the Order of the British Empire (OBE) by the British Government.

December, 1963 — lost undisputed world middleweight title to Joey Giardello in Atlantic City, New Jersey, USA.

October, 1965 — regained undisputed world middleweight title from Joey Giardello in New York, USA.

1965 — honored for a second time as "Fighter of the Year" by *The Ring* Magazine.

April, 1966 — lost undisputed world middleweight title to Emile Griffith in New York, USA.

December, 1966 — won undisputed world light heavyweight title from Jose Torres in New York, USA.

1966 — Dick Tiger is honored for a second time as "Fighter of the Year" by the Boxing Writers Association of America (BWAA).

Chronological Highlights of Dick Tiger's Life and Boxing Career

May/June 1967 — civil war breaks out in Nigeria between the federal government headed by Yakubu Gowon and the secessionist Eastern Region that took the name Republic of Biafra, led by Chukwuemeka Odumegwu-Ojukwu. Later in the year, Dick Tiger declares support for his Igbo kinsmen in their bid to secede from Nigeria as an independent state.

November, 1967 — Twelfth round of title bout in which Tiger knocks out Roger Rouse in Madison Square Garden, New York is named "Round of the Year" by *The Ring* Magazine.

May, 1968 — Dick Tiger loses light heavyweight title to Bob Foster in New York, USA: the fourth round during which Tiger suffers the first and only knock out of his career since campaigning abroad, is named "Round of the Year" by *The Ring* Magazine.

1968 — non-title bout between Dick Tiger and Frank DePaula held in New York on October 25. This is declared "Fight of the Year" by *The Ring* Magazine.

May, 1969 — Dick Tiger defeats reigning world middleweight champion, Nino Benvenuti in a non-tile fight in New York, USA.

1970 — The civil war in Nigeria ends with the defeat of the Biafran secessionists. Dick Tiger accepts defeat gallantly and without bitterness, despite having lost the bulk of his considerable assets in the country, which he had acquired from investment of his professional earnings.

July, 1970 — Dick Tiger's last professional bout is held in New York, USA. He loses a rematch against Emile Griffith by a close decision.

DICK TIGER

1971 — Dick Tiger formally retires and shortly thereafter is diagnosed as being terminally ill with liver cancer. The retired champion returns home to a reunited Nigeria where he dies on December 14 in the city of Aba, near his birthplace of Amaigbo. He passes on peacefully in the care of his family and loved ones and is buried in his birthplace.

1988 — Dick Tiger is ranked sixth by *The Ring* Magazine in its "All Time Rating of 40 World Middleweight Champions from 1886 to 1980."

1991 — Dick Tiger is inducted posthumously into the International Boxing Hall of Fame (IBHOF) at Canastota, New York.

1996 — Dick Tiger is rated first by *The Ring* Magazine in its "All Time Rating of African Born Boxers".

2001 — Dick Tiger is rated fourteenth among "The Twenty Greatest Middleweight Champions of all Time" in the January 2001 issue of *The Ring* Magazine.

The Professional Fight Record of Dick Tiger*

Year/ Date	Opponent	Fight Location	Results/ Rounds	Title
1952				
Oct	Simon Eme	Lagos, Nigeria	W, KO, rd2	-
Nov	Easy Dynamite	Lagos, Nigeria	W KO, rd1	-
Dec	Mighty Joe	Lagos, Nigeria	W, rd8	-
1953				
Jan	Lion Rose	Lagos, Nigeria	W, TKO, rd6	-
Feb	Simon Eme	Lagos, Nigeria	W, rd8	-
March	Koko Kid	Lagos, Nigeria	W, rd8	-
April	Black Power	Lagos, Nigeria	W, rd8	-
May 6	Tommy West	Lagos, Nigeria	L, TKO'd rd7	NMT
Oct	Bolaji Johnson	Lagos, Nigeria	W, rd8	-
1954				
Feb	Robert Nuanne	Lagos, Nigeria	W, Ko, rd2	-
May	Tommy West	Lagos, Nigeria	W, rd12***	NMT
July	Roy Fagbemi	Lagos, Nigeria	W, rd8	-
Nov	Peter Okpara	Lagos, Nigeria	KO, rd8	-
1955				
Jan	Koko Kid	Amaigbo, Nigeria	W, TKO, rd6	-
March	Superhuman Power	Lagos, Nigeria	W, rd8	-
May	John Ama	Lagos, Nigeria	W, KO, rd2	-
Dec 8	Alan Dean	Liverpool, England	L, rd6	-
1956				
Jan 27	Gerry McNally	Blackpool, England	L, rd8	-
March 2	Jimmy Lynas	Blackpool, England	L, rd8	-
March 22	George Roe	Liverpool, England	L, rd8	-
May 3	Dennis Rowley	Liverpool, England	W, KO, rd1	-
May 10	Alan Dean	Liverpool, England	W, rd8	-
May 28	Wally Scott	West Hartlepool, England	WTKO, rd6	-
July 2	Jimmy Lynas	West Hartlepool, England	W, rd8	-
Oct 18	Alan Dean	Liverpool, England	L, rd6	-
Nov 9	Alan Dean	Blackpool, England	W, rd8	-

DICK TIGER

1957				
April 29	Johnny Read	London, England	TKO, rd2	-
May 14	Terry Downes	London, England	TKO, rd5	-
June 4	Marius Dori	London, England	TKO, rd7	-
July 15	Willie Armstrong	West Hartlepool, England	L, rd8	-
July 25	Alan Dean	Liverpool, England,	rd8	-
Sep 9	Phil Edwards	Cardiff, Wales	W, rd10	-
Oct 21	Jean Poison	Cardiff, Wales	W, rd10	-
Nov 11	Pat McAteer	Cardiff, Wales	D, rd10	-
Nov 29	Paddy Delargy	Birmingham, England	W, TKO, rd6	-
1958				
Jan 13	Jean Ruellet	Hull, England	W, rd8	-
Feb 3	Jimmy lynas	Manchester, England	W, TKO, rd7	-
Feb 25	Johnny Read	London, England	W, TKO, rd6	-
Mar 27	Pat McAteer	Liverpool, England	W, KO, rd9	BEMT
May 1	Billy Ellaway	Liverpool, England	W, TKO, rd2	-
June 24	Spider Webb	London, England	L, rd10	-
Oct 14	Yolande Pompey	London, England	W, rd10	-
1959				
Mar 19	Randy Sandy	Liverpool, England	L, rd10	-
May 12	Randy Sandy	London, England	W, rd10	-
June 5	Rory Calhoun	New York, USA	D, rd10	-
July 17	Rory Calhoun	Syracuse, NY USA	L, rd10	-
Sep 2	Gene Armstrong	Camden, NJ USA	W, rd10	-
Sep 30	Joey Giardello	Chicago Il USA	W, rd10	-
Nov 4	Joey Giardello	Cleveland, OH USA	L, rd10	-
Dec 30	Holly Mims	Chicago, Il USA	W, rd10	-
1960				
Feb 24	Gene Armstrong	Chicago, Il USA	W, rd10	-
April 1	Victor Zalazar	Boston, MA USA	W, rd10	-
June 22	Wilf Greaves	Edmonton, Canada	L, rd15	BEMT
June 22	Wilf Greaves	Edmonton, Canada	TKO, rd9	BEMT
1961				
Feb 18	Gene Armstrong	New York, NY USA	TKO, rd9	-
April 15	Spider Webb	New York, NY USA	TKO, rd6	-
May 15	Hank Casey	New Orleans, MSUSA	W, rd10	-
Dec 16	Bill Pickett	New York, NY USA	W, rd10	-

The Professional Fight Record of Dick Tiger

1962				
Jan 20	Floro Fernandez	Miami Beach, FL USA	KO, rd6	-
March 31	Henry Hank	New York, NY USA	W, rd10	-
Oct 23	Gene Fullmer	San Francisco CA USA	W, rd15	NBA WMT
1963				
Feb 23	Gene Fullmer	Las Vegas NV USA	D, rd15	NBA/WMT
Aug 10	Gene Fullmer	Ibadan, Nigeria	W, TKO, rd7	WMT
Dec 7	Joey Giardello	Atlantic City, NJ USA	L, rd15	UWMT
1964				
July 31	Jose Gonzalez	New York, NY USA	TKO, rd6	-
Sep 11	Don Fullmer	Cleveland, OH USA	W, rd10	-
Oct 16	Joey Archer	New York, NY USA	L, rd10	-
1965				
July 31	Rocky Rivero	New York, NY USA	TKO, rd6	-
May 20	Rubin Carter	New York NY USA	W, rd10	-
Oct 21	Joey Giardello	New York NY USA	W, rd15	WMT
1966				
Feb 18	Peter Mueller	Dortmund, Germany	W, KO, rd3	-
April 25	Emile Griffith	New York NY USA	L, rd15	UWMT
Dec 16	Jose Torres	New York NY USA	W, rd15	WLHT
1967				
Feb 5	Abraham Tonica	Port Harcourt, Nigeria	W, rd10	-
May 16	Jose Torres	Las Vegas NV USA	W, rd15	UWLHT
Nov 17	Roger Rouse	New York NY USA	W, TKO, rd12	UWLHT
1968				
May 24	Bob Foster	New York NY USA	L. KO'd, rd4	WLHT
Oct 25	Frank DePaula	New York NY USA	W, rd10	-
1969				
May 26	Nino Benvenuti	New York NY USA	W, rd10	-
Nov 14	Andy Kendall	New York NY USA	W, rd10	-
1970				
July 15	Emile Griffith	New York NY USA	L, rd10	-

DICK TIGER

Explanatory Notes

W: Won L: Lost
KO: Knock Out
rd: round in which bout ended
TKO: Technical Knock Out
TKO'd by: Loss by Technical Knock Out
NMT: Nigerian National Middleweight Title
BEMT: British Empire (later Commonwealth) Middleweight Title
NBAWMT: National Boxing Association (Later World Boxing Association) World Middleweight Title
UWMT: Undisputed World Middleweight Title
UWLHT: Undisputed World Light Heavyweight Title
*** Bouts with now contested fight results since the original edition of this biography

Cumulative Fight Statistics: Wins-61, Losses-17, Draws-3 Knockouts- 26, Total Bouts-81

* *The Boxing Register, Official Record Book of the International Boxing Hall of Fame (IBHOF)* is the source of the above listing of Tiger's professional fights, which also tallied with the records of most other sources at the time of the release of the first edition of this biography in 2002. However, during the research into the subject, the author consulted New Jersey based Ralph Citro, who has earned the reputation of being one of boxing's most competent and experienced record keepers. Citro expressed a skeptical view as regards the list. According to him, there may be at least six professional bouts that Tiger engaged in during the early stages of his career in Nigeria, the records of which might never have been properly documented or have been lost. Hence these six fights may

*The Professional Fight Record of Dick Tiger**

have been unwittingly excluded from the commonly cited list above. Furthermore, in more recent times there have been continuing contestations of the accuracy of the IBHOF list by other observers, based on ostensibly newly conducted research. Accordingly, some authorities including BoxRec - boxrec.com (stated on its website as the official record keeper of the sport of boxing) have revised the IBHOF list and reversed at least the result of one significant fight from a victory to a loss i.e. Tiger's return bout against Tommy West of May 1954, thereby suggesting that Tiger never won the Nigerian middleweight title, as originally claimed. In all, at the time of the publication of this New Edition, the IBHOF has a revised fight record for Tiger published on its website at the following url: http:// www.ibhof.com/pages/about/inductees/modern/tiger.html   making no mention of the Nigerian middle weight title and providing an amended cumulative fight results for Tiger as follows:

Total Bouts: 81
Won: 59
Lost: 19
Drew: 3
KOs: 26

Richard Ihetu aka Dick Tiger (1929-1971) World Middleweight Champion (1963 and 1965-66) and World Light Heavyweight Champion (1966-68)

Chapter One

ORIGINS AND EARLY PROFESSIONAL CAREER

Dick Tiger was born Richard Ihetu on August 14, 1929. His birthplace, Amaigbo (also referred to as Nkwerre-Orlu) was a small rural village located in the old Orlu province in the heartland of Nigeria's Igbo ethnic group situated in the southeastern region of the country, which at the time was a British West African colonial territory. His father, Ubuagwu Ihetu is said to have been a descendant of traditional Igbo wrestlers on both maternal and paternal sides of the family tree. However, about the time of Richard's birth, Ubuagwu was a rustic chicken farmer who tended free-range poultry and eked out a modest existence supported by an extended family system. The young Richard thus grew up amid his siblings and Igbo kinsmen under considerably humble conditions. During his early adolescent years, Ubuagwu died and in accordance with the customs of the time, Richard and his brothers were fostered out to their late father's relations who thereafter were responsible for their upbringing.

Richard Ihetu's early life during the 1930s and 40s, a period of nationalist struggle for the emerging Nigerian nation was largely undocumented. The poor chicken farmer's son received very little schooling and is reputed to have gravitated towards his boxing profession more by sheer circumstances rather than by any grand design. Lacking any real formal education, the career options opened to him were minimal. By 1950, the year he turned 21, Richard had done little else other than menial work for various masters, including officers of the British colonial authorities stationed in the environs of his homeland. Uzoma Onyemaechi of the University of Michigan, Ann Arbor states (in his web site highlighting the Igbo People) that the young Ihetu was a "bottle picker" at the Eke Oha market in Aba Township between 1951 and 1952, during which time he also doubled as a retailer, engaging in petty trading. Amid the hectic commercial activities of the Aba market, Richard sold his empty bottles, and various other household goods and utensils as well as pet monkeys and parrots procured from Opobo, the vibrant commercial center in the coastal part of what is now known as Rivers State in the Niger Delta region, homeland of the historically renowned legendary merchant trader and later King Jaja. In the often chaotic environment of the Aba market, the young Richard regularly took on the role of an "enforcer" of order. During incessant water shortages long queues of townspeople formed around the public water pumps of the marketplace, collecting water. The young Richard was among the youth engaged by the local authorities to maintain order, controlling and warding off the unruly ruffians and miscreants who threatened the smooth running of the process.

It was this initial public display of physical strength and combativeness that earned for Richard the recognition of his nascent pugilistic skills by the local authorities, which would ultimately lead his path on to a profession in boxing. These

Origins and Early Professional Career

skills (which would serve him very well in later life) were first spotted by some of the resident British colonial army officers in the region who thereafter encouraged him to take up boxing as a profession. Following a brief and largely unrecorded amateur boxing career, Richard Ihetu turned professional as a middleweight in 1952 at the age of 23.

The initial financial rewards of the young Richard's new boxing profession were however only marginally better than that of the menial tasks and petty trading he had hitherto done. He thus had to continue with the humble labors to supplement the meager earnings from his boxing career. Nationally renowned Nigerian sports administrator and labor union leader, late Chief Ganiyu Kolawole Balogun was one of the young boxer's mentors at the time and he confirmed to the author in an interview in 1995, the very humble conditions under which Tiger's professional boxing career began. In 1954, Balogun facilitated Richard's move from his rural eastern home base to the more cosmopolitan city of Ibadan in Nigeria's Western Region and he housed the fighter in the "boys quarters" of his home, a dwelling customarily meant for underlings and servants. By night, the young Tiger worked as a night watchman at the country's first privately owned stadium and trained during the day for his fights against the local competition. All his early professional bouts, with the exception of one, took place at the colonial territory's rapidly urbanizing capital city of Lagos, lying some 90 miles south of Ibadan on the Atlantic coast.

The IBHOF records show that in 1952, Tiger's first year as a professional boxer, he fought three times, registering two consecutive knockouts on to his professional log. In his professional debut in October he dispatched his opponent,

Simon Eme in two rounds and the following month Tiger knocked out his second opponent simply listed as "Easy Dynamite" in the opening round. The future World champion's third professional fight was held in December of same year. The opponent this time was one "Mighty Joe" who took Tiger the full length of the scheduled 8-round bout, but nonetheless, lost by decision to the future champion.

Having fought an average of a bout a month in the last quarter of the opening year of his professional career, Tiger fought a total of six bouts the following year, all of which took place in Lagos. The year, 1953 opened for the rising contender with a knockout victory over "Lion Rose" (listed as "Lion Ring" by other sources) in six rounds in January. He was rematched against Simon Eme in February of the year and this time the opponent lasted until the closing bell of the 8- round bout, albeit suffering a second loss to Tiger by decision. The next two opponents on Tiger's IBHOF fight log, "Koko Kid" and "Black Power" (or "Blackie Power", as referred to in other sources) were also to take Tiger the full distance of scheduled 8-round bouts, though the fighter from Amaigbo would remain undefeated. However, his winning ways were soon to end abruptly.

With a record of only seven professional fights, Tiger was matched against Tommy West for the Nigerian middleweight title on May 6, 1953. After putting up a good fight for six rounds, Tiger lost by a technical knockout in the seventh. Sources including Boxrec.com have indicated he had to discontinue the fight due to an injured thumb. He was not to fight again for almost half a year to allow the broken thumb to heal properly. During this time his handlers took him back to training camp to prepare him for a successful return to the ring.

Origins and Early Professional Career

Well rested, better trained and in top form, Tiger was back in the ring in October 1953 to outpoint respected Lagosian contender Bolaji Johnson in eight rounds. In February 1954 he knocked out Robert Nuanne in two rounds, moving his professional record up to nine wins and only one loss. He was now set to meet his former conqueror Tommy West again, in a second bid for the Nigerian middleweight championship title. A year after the first title bout, the two engaged in a war of attrition in Lagos in May 1954. The results of the fight (as earlier pointed out in the revised fight record in this New Edition) are now a subject of controversy. The original IBHOF records had indicated that Tiger outfought West in the rematch, avenging his earlier loss by a points decision victory and winning the Nigerian 160 pound middleweight title in the process. However, according to Boxrec.com recent research has now suggested that Tiger was again defeated by West and thus really never won the Nigerian middleweight title. Whatever the case, all sources are unanimous in that Dick Tiger would never lose again while fighting professionally in his Nigerian homeland.

Before the end of 1954, two additional wins were added to Tiger's fight record. He outpointed Roy Fagbemi in July, two months after the controversial rematch with West. Four months thereafter, Tiger knocked out another opponent, Peter Okpara in eight rounds. During the following year i.e., 1955, Dick Tiger was to reach the first crucial point of his fighting career. His reputation as a talented middleweight boxer was now growing rapidly. He overcame the challenge of an old adversary, Koko Kid, by a sixth round technical knockout in his hometown of Amaigbo in January, treating his townsfolk to an exciting exhibition of his rugged fighting skills. An opponent listed as "Super Human Power" in the record books lasted the full length of an 8- round bout against Tiger in Lagos in March of the same year. Nonetheless the champion was victorious over the hyperbolically named challenger.

Tiger's next fight, against John Ama, would be his last in Nigeria for over a decade, according to the IBHOF records. Ama was defeated after only two rounds in which Tiger completely dominated his challenger. Tiger had now piled up an impressive fight record in the boxing ring which had not gone unnoticed by the close observers of the development of the sport in the colonial territory. Jack Farnsworth, British insurance salesman and a keen promoter of the sport, who would later be credited for the establishment of the Nigerian Boxing Board of Control (NBBC), had followed closely the budding career of the stocky five foot eight inch Nigerian fighter, highly enthralled by Tiger's rise to national prominence in the country's boxing arena. Greatly impressed by Tiger's string of victories and convinced of his potential, Farnsworth arranged to have the Nigerian middleweight contender move over to England to continue his fighting career under experienced trainer, Peter Benencko. In the summer of 1955, aged 26, Tiger bade farewell to his beloved homeland and set sail for Liverpool following a tradition of transatlantic migration of African boxers to the Western world.

Chapter Two

LIVERPOOL: FIGHTER IN A STRANGE LAND

Adjusting to life in his new environment in Liverpool, England was a grueling and tasking process for the now 26 year- old Richard Ihetu. As the summer season gave way to winter, he found the great difference in weather from his tropical homeland difficult to bear. The severe cold and windy English climate was a sharp contrast to the high humidity and sizzling heat of Nigeria, which lay deep in the West African rain forest. However, the determined Richard would not let the adverse climatic conditions deter him from staying focused on achieving his goal of becoming a world-class boxer. He endured the discomforts he suffered and made the most of the improved facilities available to him in his new environment by training hard and diligently under his new handlers.

However, the inclement weather was not the only problem Tiger faced in his new surroundings. He soon also found that he needed to adjust to the British style of boxing, which laid less emphasis on raw aggression than on savvy and defensive skills. On December 8, 1955, he fought and was defeated in his first fight abroad, a decision loss to Alan Dean in Liverpool. In 1956

Tiger's resolve to excel in his fistic profession was severely tested as he lost bout after bout by decision. On January 27, and March 2, 1956, respectively, Gerry McNally and Jimmy Lynas were awarded victories over the transplanted Nigerian in middleweight bouts held in Blackpool. Subsequently, a fourth opponent, George Roe, also went away with a decision win over Tiger in a middleweight bout fought on March 22, 1956, in Liverpool. These repeated decision losses seemed to have convinced the future champion that he had to prove his mettle by scoring knockouts over his British opponents and not leaving the prerogative of deciding the outcome of his bouts to the referees and judges to make.

Accordingly in his fifth fight abroad held on May 3, 1956, back in Liverpool, Tiger made sure to knock out his opponent, Dennis Rowley, within the first round. He may not yet have fully acquired the savvy and sophistication which the British style laid emphasis on, but with his unrelenting aggression and ruggedness, he more than made up for this deficiency. Still, the Nigerian fighter was also learning some of the underlying rudiments and finer points of his brutal sport from consistent training and listening attentively to his trainers and handlers. In his next bout he displayed some of these finer points, in addition of course to his usual intense aggressiveness. He was thus able to win a decision over Alan Dean in a rematch held in Liverpool just a week after the Rowley knockout.

Fighting a third time in the month of May, 1956, Tiger knocked out Wally Scott in four rounds in West Hartlepool. Two months later, on July 2, back again in the same county of Northeast England, the Nigerian avenged his previous loss to Jimmy Lynas by outpointing the Briton over eight rounds. Tiger then fought a pair of bouts against another

Liverpool: Fighter in a Strange Land

former opponent, Alan Dean, the first fighter he had fought upon arriving in England. At Liverpool on October 18, 1956, he got the short end of another points decision against the Briton in a 6- round bout but three weeks later, Tiger reversed the loss, emerging victorious over Dean in an 8-round bout fought in Blackpool. By the end of 1956, Tiger's fight record included at least six losses. His quest to achieve world acclaim in boxing was turning out quite precarious and by no means, certain. Nonetheless he remained unwavering in his commitment to the tasks ahead and in his belief that he would eventually find his footing. Time would ultimately prove him right.

1957 was to be a very busy year for the future world champion during which he engaged in a total of nine professional bouts. The caliber of the opponents he fought became tougher and the British boxing authorities and fans alike began to sense that their Nigerian invader was destined for greatness. It was at this time that Richard Ihetu was christened with his fighting name of "Dick Tiger", "Dick", being the shortened form of his first name of Richard and "Tiger" taken to symbolize his ferocity in the boxing ring. In the eyes of the boxing fans that had trooped out en masse to watch his action-packed fights, he had done enough to earn the moniker.

Dick Tiger's first three bouts in 1957 were held in London, and all were knockout victories for him. Among his victims was Terry Downes, a future world champion himself, who suffered a fifth round technical knockout at the fists of the Tiger on May 14, 1957. Before the victory over Downes, Tiger had stopped Johnny Read in two rounds on April 29, and subsequently, Marius Dori surrendered to the Tiger in the seventh round on June 4th of the same year.

However, Dick Tiger's winning streak was again to be halted abruptly. On July 15, 1957, he lost a decision to tough Willie Armstrong at West Hartlepool. Undaunted by the loss, Tiger shook off the stigma of the temporary setback and campaigned on with even greater vigor. Barely a fortnight after the loss to Armstrong in West Hartlepool, the Nigerian prizefighter was back in Liverpool facing a familiar opponent, Alan Dean, for the fifth time. Dean now had the edge of having won two of their previous four fights and drawn with him in one. In the fifth duel however, the Briton was outpointed by Tiger over eight rounds.

Up next on Tiger's fight itinerary was Cardiff Wales, where he engaged in the first official 10-round bout of his career on September 9, 1957. His opponent, Phil Edwards put up a gallant struggle, but the judges ruled in favor of Tiger. The Nigerian returned to the Welsh capital later in the same year for his next two bouts, winning another ten round points decision over Jean Poison and fighting Pat McAteer to a draw on October 21 and November 11 respectively. The year ended with Tiger registering another impressive professional knockout. Suffering the casualty was Paddy Delargy, who was battered into submission in the sixth of a 10-round bout, held on November 29 in Birmingham.

1958 may be considered the year in which the boxing career of Dick Tiger finally reached the milestone that would lead him on to the pinnacle of the sport. His first bout of the year was held in the Northeastern English port city of Hull on January 13. Tiger won an 8 round bout against Jean Ruellet by decision and moved on to Manchester the following month where he finally knocked out an old foe, Jimmy Lynas, whom he had battled against on two previous occasions. Another old opponent, Johnny Read, whom Tiger had beaten in two rounds in 1957, was then given the opportunity of avenging his loss to the Tiger. Read fought the rising Nigerian star on February 25th of that year and suffered yet another defeat via a sixth round technical knockout when the referee mercifully halted the one-sided fight in Tiger's favor. The time was now ripe for Tiger to raise his status as a dominant fighter within the British Isles to that of a champion of the entire British Commonwealth.

On March 27, 1958, Dick Tiger and another former opponent, Peter McAteer (against whom Tiger had drawn in a 1957 bout) fought for the British Empire middleweight title in Liverpool. The hard fought battle ended in the ninth round with McAteer suffering a technical knockout and Tiger emerging as the new British Empire middleweight champion. Finally, the years of dedicated training and personal sacrifice were beginning to pay off for the Nigerian boxer. Riding the crest of his newly won title, he knocked out Billy Ellaway in two rounds on May Day 1958 in Liverpool. Tiger's subsequent bouts of the year would be against two American fighters ranked in the top ten of the ratings of the National Boxing Association (NBA), Spider Webb and Yolande Pompey. Webb won a decision over Tiger over a 10-round bout fought in London on June 24, 1958, while the Nigerian outpointed Pompey over same number of rounds in the same city on October 14.

As 1958 ended, Tiger's professional fight log according to the IBHOF had stacked up to a total of 42 bouts, comprising 33 wins (including 18 knockouts) and eight losses. He had graduated into a seasoned professional with Commonwealth laurels to his credit. However, he still had some way to go in his quest for a world title and ultimately international acclaim. For the rising Nigerian boxer, 1959 was to be another decisive year during which time he would cross over from England to America to continue his quest for boxing's golden fleece. However, before the move to America, Tiger fought a pair of bouts against another American top contender, Randy Sandy in England. On March 22, 1959, in Liverpool, he lost a 10-round decision to Sandy and on May 12 of the same year, avenged the loss by winning a 10- round points decision in London.

Also, before his relocation to America from England, the future champion took time off from his busy fight schedule and returned to his Nigerian homeland to fulfill an important personal goal he had been nursing for a while—to get married to his hometown sweetheart— Abigail Ogbuji—whom he had been courting for a while. The champion-in-waiting and his pretty bride were joined together in holy matrimony at a simple, but happy ceremony in Amaigbo attended by close family members and long-standing friends. Abigail would be a faithful wife and Tiger's life-long partner as well as a great source of inspiration and support to him in all his future endeavors, standing staunchly by him through all the trials and tribulations that were to come. Towards the end of year, Abigail gave birth to twins, presenting Tiger with a baby girl and a baby boy much to his joy. The couple was later blessed with six other children: three girls and three boys. All eight siblings would enjoy the complete devotion and support of their loving parents.

Chapter Three

TIGER IN AMERICA

Dick Tiger moved to the United States and began his eleven-year boxing campaign in America from midyear of 1959, under the guidance of Willis "Jersey" Jones, a seasoned fight manager. As was the case with the Nigerian boxer's experience in England, he was to find that establishing himself among the ranks of the top middleweights of the day in America would be a tough challenge. His early bouts in the US were not auspicious and hardly indicative of the international success that he would later win. In his US debut, Tiger fought Rory Calhoun on June 5, 1959 in New York City and was only able to eke out a draw against the top-ten contender. In a rematch held in Syracuse the following month, the American was awarded a decision over Tiger.

Tiger finally scored his first victory on American soil on September 2, 1959, in Camden, New Jersey - a 10-round decision win over Gene Armstrong, another top-ten middleweight contender. His next opponent was Joey Giardello, whom Tiger would come to know quite well in the years ahead. Both men would engage in a total of four bouts, two of which would be for the world middleweight title. For the moment however,

Tiger emerged victorious by the judges' decision in this first encounter, a 10-round non-title bout held on September 30, 1959, in Chicago.

Asked to recall his memories of the late Tiger in an interview conducted by *The Ring* Magazine in late 1996 for an article commemorating the 25th anniversary of Tiger's death in January 1997, Giardello noted, "He [Tiger] was one of the best. I know because I fought him four times. I was one of the first guys he fought when he came over from England [in 1959]. I didn't think much of him. I didn't train that hard, and he beat me. He was very strong. And a gentleman. One thing I always remember about him: If you hit him low, he didn't complain about it like the fighters of today. He was a real professional."

Both future champions fought again three months after their first bout, with Giardello awarded a points victory over Tiger in the rematch held on November 4, 1959, in Cleveland, Ohio. The judges' nod went to the quick-footed American after ten rounds of a cautiously fought bout in which each adversary showed the other considerable respect. For Tiger, 1959 came to a close with his record at 37 wins and 11 defeats, after he outpointed Holly Mimms, another American top-ten contender over a 10-round bout held in Chicago the day before new year's eve. The following year, i.e. 1960 was a particularly special one for the Tiger. His Nigerian homeland, in which he had shown much pride, and where he had become a national hero, attained nationhood, gaining its national independence from its former colonial "master", Britain.

On February 24, 1960, Gene Armstrong, who had been relegated from the top-ten ratings following his loss to Tiger the year before, sought vengeance against the Nigerian in a rematch held in Chicago. However, Tiger comfortably won the 10-round bout by decision. He proceeded to Boston on April 1 of the same year to outpoint Victor Zalazar in another 10-round bout. Tiger's third fight of 1960 would be in defense of his British Empire middleweight title. The championship bout was held in Edmonton, Alberta Canada on June 22. At the conclusion of the scheduled 15 rounds, the challenger, Wilf Greaves was deemed by the judges as having done enough to be awarded the title.

However, the dethroned champion returned to the Canadian city to reclaim the title barely six months later. On November 30, 1960, Tiger won a decisive victory over Greaves via a ninth round technical knockout. The Nigerian Independence Day which had been celebrated a month earlier on October 1, served as a great motivation for Tiger in ensuring that he was reinstated British Empire champion. And quite naturally Tiger's victory was cause for further celebration by his Nigerian countrymen and women who had been basking in a state of national euphoria since the October independence festivities marking the end of about a century of British colonial rule.

Indeed, Nigeria's national independence had been greeted by both its nationals and the world at large with great optimism. The independence ceremony took place with much pomp and pageantry in the country's capital city of Lagos as Nigeria's newly elected government proudly hosted members of the British royalty, top officials of the ruling British Labor Party government and the international community at large. As a sovereign nation, Nigeria held out the potentials for greatness in world affairs, being the most populous country in Africa, and one of the richest on the continent in both human and mineral resources.

The increased sense of pride and enhanced self-esteem for black people the world over, through Nigeria's independence, was not lost on Dick Tiger. The auspicious development tremendously boosted his ego and will to excel. He would not lose a single bout in the following two years (i.e., 1961 and 1962). In the former year, he exploded as a major force in the international middleweight division and within the following year, he won and eventually unified the hitherto split world middleweight title.

Gene Armstrong who had lost two previous decisions to Tiger was his first victim in 1961. The two boxers fought for a third time on February 18th in New York City. Fight fans were finally convinced of the Nigerian's superiority over the American when Tiger bullied Armstrong for nine rounds, prompting the referee into effecting a stoppage of the bout and awarding Tiger a ninth round technical knockout. Spider Webb, another aspiring American middleweight contender, who had defeated Tiger on points in London in 1958, was next on Tiger's "hit list". The Tiger - Webb rematch took place on April 15, 1961, in the Saint Nicholas Arena, New York. Following a fast paced exchange of hostilities in the early rounds, Tiger connected Webb with a furious two-punch combination of left and right to the head in the sixth round, sending the American to the canvass on all fours. Webb somehow managed to beat the count, but a subsequent wicked left hook delivered to his jaw by Tiger ended the fight. It was the first technical knockout that Webb had suffered in 40 professional fights.

Tiger's two fights for the remainder of the year were also clear victories for him. He won a 10-round decision over American top-ten contender, Hank Casey, in New Orleans on May 15, 1961 and took a seven- month break before also outpointing Bill Pickett over ten rounds in New York. The Nigerian boxer was well on his way to claiming the world title and winning international acclaim. 1962 would be the decisive year for Tiger, during which the stage would be set for him to become Africa's most accomplished boxer in the modern era of the sport.

Tiger's first opponent in the landmark year was hard punching Cuban top contender, Florentino Fernandez, who had nearly dethroned Gene Fullmer the reigning world middleweight champion in August of 1961. Seeking to re-establish himself and earn another shot at the world title, the 26 year old Fernandez decided to take on Tiger, who by now had earned recognition as the world's number one middleweight contender. The two top contenders squared off in Miami Beach, Florida on January 20, 1962, with the winner all but assured of being the next to challenge the world champion.

Aware of Fernandez' own reputation as a solid puncher, the usually quick starting Tiger boxed cautiously for five rounds, leaving the main thrust of the aggression to his Cuban opponent. The cautious strategy of minimizing his own risk while looking to capitalize on counter punches eventually paid off for Tiger in the sixth round. About halfway into the round, Fernandez threw a furious left hook, which Tiger artfully evaded, moving stealthily out of the range of the Cuban's missile. As Fenandez' fist swung harmlessly past his head, Tiger countered with a powerful chopping right cross that landed squarely on Fernadez' nose, splitting it wide open. Bloodied and badly hurt with a broken nose, the Cuban boldly tried to fight on but the ringside doctor advised the referee to halt the fight and Tiger was awarded a sixth round technical knockout.

However, before Tiger would secure a challenge of the world champion, he also fought another top-ten contender,

Henry Hank in New York barely two months after the victory over Fernandez. On March 31, 1962, the thirty-two year old Nigerian won a 10-round decision over his American opponent. Tiger was finally set to cross over the threshold and make his bid for the world title.

Chapter Four

ENTER THE TIGER: THE FIRST WORLD CHAMPIONSHIP REIGN

The first of Dick Tiger's three world championship reigns began in California's famous Candlestick Park in San Francisco on October 23, 1962. After a hard fought world title bout that went the full 15-round distance, Tiger was awarded a unanimous decision win over the NBA champion, Gene Fullmer. At the end of the encounter the dethroned champion's face was so bloody and badly cut from Tiger's punches to the head during the fight that the decision was a foregone conclusion. Even before the official announcement of Tiger's decisive victory, a large congregation of Nigerians in attendance lifted their hero onto their shoulders in the ring-center in national jubilation. Among them was the country's first world champion, Hogan "Kid" Bassey (featherweight champion from 1957 to 1958). Dick Tiger, the fighter from Amaigbo had become a symbol of national pride for the new Nigerian nation and an avalanche of accolades came pouring in for him from all over the country.

Three months after defeating Fullmer, the former champion was granted a rematch by Tiger in his first title defense. It was now early 1963 and both *The Ring* Magazine and the Boxing Writers Association of America (BWAA) had named the Nigerian as the "Fighter of the Year" for 1962. The Tiger—Fullmer rematch took place in Las Vegas, Nevada on February 23, 1963, with the current and immediate past NBA world middleweight titleholders fighting to an inconclusive 15- round draw. The unsatisfactory result of the rematch led to a third and final encounter between the two fighters, finally putting an end to the controversy over who the real champion was.

Jack Solomons, legendary British boxing promoter of the 50s and 60s, arranged for the third match between the NBA champion and his predecessor to be held in Ibadan, Nigeria, capitalizing on the nationalistic fervor in Tiger's newly independent homeland and the Nigerian boxer's increasing international popularity. This was the same southwestern city where about a decade earlier Tiger had toiled in obscurity to make a name for himself in his chosen professional sport. The fight was held at the newly constructed Liberty Stadium, an impressive Olympic-size sports facility built as a monument to the country's recently acquired status as a free nation. On August 10, 1963, the scheduled date of the fight, Nigerian dignitaries from all over the country joined the multitude of fight fans that jam-packed the fight venue to watch their "champion" defend his title against the American challenger.

Veteran American journalist Lloyd Garrison noted while writing on the fight in the *New York Times* some years later "It was pandemonium that night at Liberty Stadium." "Everyone who counted [in the country]" he reported, "was at ringside." Among the large retinue of Nigerian VIPs in attendance was the internationally renowned nationalist and the country's first indigenous Governor-General and later President, the

Enter the Tiger: The First World Championship Reign

Honorable Dr. Nnamdi Azikiwe, who was a fellow Igbo kinsman of the world champion.

Under the circumstances and given the great expectations of his countrymen and women, it would have been something just short of a national disaster had Dick Tiger failed to deliver on his home turf. However, Tiger totally dominated the former champion turned challenger throughout the duration of the title bout, forcing a premature ending to the final encounter. Fullmer surrendered after six brutal onesided rounds in what would be the last fight of the rugged American's boxing career. However, despite the humiliating career-ending defeat Fullmer suffered, he bore no malice against his conqueror and only held him in the highest regard given the congenial manner Tiger had comported himself.

Commenting on his defeat nearly two and a half decades later, on the 25th anniversary of Tiger's death in 1997, Fullmer said of his successor: "If I was gonna lose to somebody, I can't think of anyone I would rather have lost to than Tiger. He was a very courageous fighter, and as cordial a man as anyone I've ever met. When I fought him in Nigeria, he was gracious, and I was treated as well as anywhere else I ever fought—and maybe better." In concluding his personal tribute to his successor, Fullmer stated unequivocally "Whenever I 'm asked about the best fighters I ever faced, I always put Tiger right up there."

With the victory over Fullmer in Ibadan, Nigeria, Dick Tiger's stature grew from that of a national symbol into that of an internationally acclaimed sports hero. Boxing's three other main regional and international controlling bodies, (i.e., the New York State Athletic Commission (NYAC), the European Boxing Union (EBU) and the British Boxing Board of Control (BBBC) all joined the National Boxing Association (NBA) in recognizing Tiger as the legitimate world middleweight champion making him the undisputed title-holder. To cap this enviable achievement and in testimony to the international acclaim and respect he had earned, the British government also bestowed Tiger with membership in the Order of the British Empire (OBE), an honor usually bestowed only on outstanding international statesmen and notable national figures. Indeed, the year of 1963 was a glorious one for the Nigerian world champion, who was now in the eleventh year of his professional boxing career.

However, Tiger's first championship reign was to be quite brief. In his very next fight after the second victory over Fullmer, Tiger lost his world middleweight title to his old adversary, Joey Giardello. Both fighters, who had split a pair of ten round decisions in non-title bouts, fought their third bout for the world title on December 7, 1963, in Atlantic City, New Jersey. After fifteen rounds of tactical fighting on the part of both protagonists, Giardello was declared winner by a close decision and thus awarded the title. The decision was made by the sole judge, referee Paul Cavalier - ruling in favor of the more mobile challenger, whose punches were deemed as sharper and more accurate than the dethroned champion's. Dick Tiger had lost the world title after only three title defenses!

The loss of the world title after the relatively brief period of having held it was naturally a great disappointment for the dethroned Tiger. However, the hardy Nigerian fighter was certainly not about to throw in the towel and end his boxing career yet. After all, he was not new to rebounding from defeat just when the pundits had given up on him. He immediately set his mind on regaining the championship and began working towards securing a rematch against Giardello, a goal for which he channeled all his energy and training. However, the former world champion had to wait patiently for nearly two years. During this time, he re-established himself among the top contenders of the day, and invariably could not be denied the opportunity of regaining his lost title.

Six months after the loss to Giardello, Dick Tiger returned to the ring to face Jose Gonzalez in New York City on July 31, 1964. The Nigerian former world champion won a clear victory over the Hispanic contender via a sixth round technical knockout. Another two months down the road, in September, Gene Fullmer's younger brother, Don took on Tiger in Cleveland, Ohio seeking to accomplish what his older sibling had failed to do in three bouts against Tiger (i.e., to defeat the Nigerian). After the two brawled for ten rounds, the judges ruled in favor of Tiger awarding him his fiftieth victory in a total of 67 professional bouts.

Tiger's comeback suffered a temporary setback in October of 1964 when top-ten rated American contender, Joey Archer, was awarded a close decision over the Nigerian at the conclusion of a 10-round bout held in New York City. The former champion redeemed himself of this loss by scoring decisive victories in his next two fights. On March 12, 1965, he easily defeated perennial Argentine journeyman contender, Rocky "Roly Poly" Rivero in New York by a sixth round technical knockout. Next up for Tiger was highly rated American contender, Rubin "Hurricane" Carter who was also seeking an opportunity to challenge for the world title. It was generally assumed that the winner between the two would be the one to challenge Giardello in the champion's next title defense.

The Tiger-Carter elimination bout was held on May 20, 1965, at Madison Square Garden, New York City, which had by then acquired the status of the world's premier fight venue. In a particularly vicious battle, Tiger scored three knock downs of the highly regarded Carter en route to a decision victory over the American. There could now be no denying the Nigerian former champion the opportunity to regain his lost crown. He was about to re-write boxing history by joining Tony Zale and Sugar Ray Robinson, two great champions of the past, as the only men who had successfully regained the world middleweight title after losing it.

Photographs

The British Empire (Commonwealth) Middleweight Champion and rising world title contender poses in the gym in Liverpool England, (circa 1959)

A publicity shot of the Middleweight World Champion winking at the camera shortly after first winning the title from Gene Fullmer in 1962

Photographs

Liberty Stadium Ibadan, Nigeria — Tiger and Gene Fullmer get set for their third and final world title fight held on August 10, 1963. With them is Nigerian Minister of Labor, Welfare and Sports, Chief Joseph Modupe Johnson CFR

DICK TIGER

Tale of the Tape: Gene Fullmer Versus Dick Tiger for the NBA World Middleweight Title in San Francisco, California August 1963.

Photographs

Nigerian fight fans carry Dick Tiger shoulder high at ring center celebrating the victory of their countryman over Gene Fullmer for the NBA World Middleweight Title, Candlestick Park, San Francisco October 1962

Tiger with the ill-fated Featherweight World Champion, Davey Moore receive Merit Award from the Boxing Writers Association of America (BWAA) in New York, February 1963. Just a month later the Featherweight Champion died shortly after suffering a knockout defeat from his successor, Sugar Ramos

World Middleweight Champion, Dick Tiger and number one contender, Joey Giardello pose for a publicity shot prior to the third of their four encounters in December 1963.

Photographs

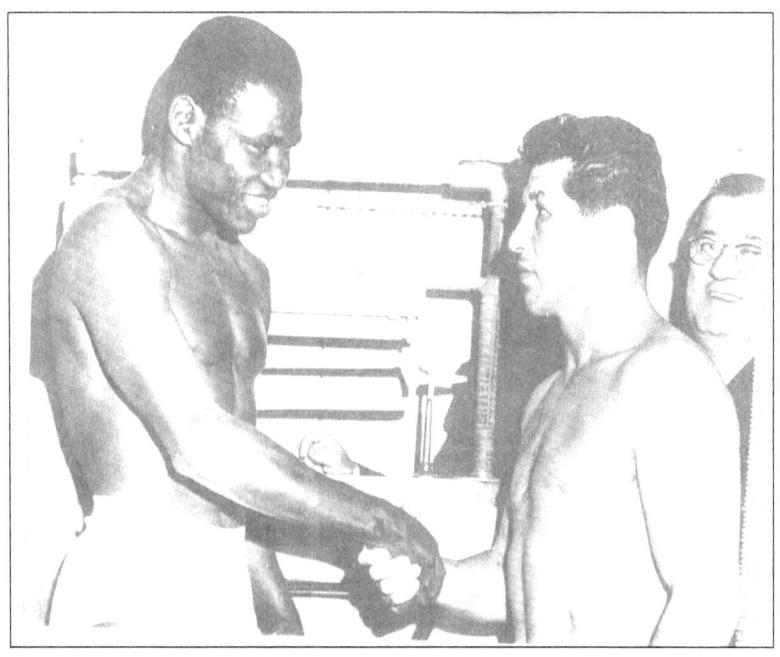

Tiger and Giardello in a handshake at the weigh in for their 1963 World title fight

DICK TIGER

Tale of the Tape: Dick Tiger versus Joey Giardello for the undisputed world middleweight title in Atlantic City, New Jersey U.S.A. December 7 1963.

Photographs

In a publicity shot arranged to celebrate the occasion of his 34th birthday in August 1963, Tiger is hand fed a piece of cake by his ever-loving wife, Abigail, (Courtesy, *The Daily Times* of Nigeria)

The Tiger and his wife Abigail dance at a celebratory event in Lagos circa 1964 (Courtesy, *The Daily Times* of Nigeria)

Photographs

Circa September 1963: Friends, well-wishers, fans and family are regaled by the World Middleweight Champion following a toast in honor of his 34th birthday at a cocktail party held in Lagos. First on the left is his dear wife, Abigail. (Courtesy *The Daily Times* of Nigeria)

From one Legend to Another: Longest ever reigning World Heavyweight Champion, Joe Louis (1937- 1949) lends a hand holding the heavy bag for Dick Tiger during a training session (circa 1963).

Photographs

The Tiger training on an exercise cycle in preparation for a fight, circa 1964

Rubin "Hurricane" Carter is down for the count after fielding a devastating two-punch combination from Tiger during a nontitle bout at the legendary New York Madison Square Garden, May 20, 1965.

Circa 1964: *The Ring* Magazine's championship belt is presented to Dick Tiger in Lagos by the Nigerian Minister of Labor, Welfare and Sports, Chief J.M. Johnson CFR on behalf of *The Ring* Publisher, Nat Fleischer (Courtesy, *The Daily Times* of Nigeria).

Representative of Queen Elizabeth II of England presents Dick Tiger with a plaque commemorating the award of the Order of the British Empire (OBE) on him by the British Government in 1963. (Courtesy, *The Daily Times* of Nigeria)

Circa 1964: A novelty publicity shot to promote an upcoming bout; Tiger parries the right hook of a gloved model before the World Press in London. (Courtesy, *The Daily Times* of Nigeria)

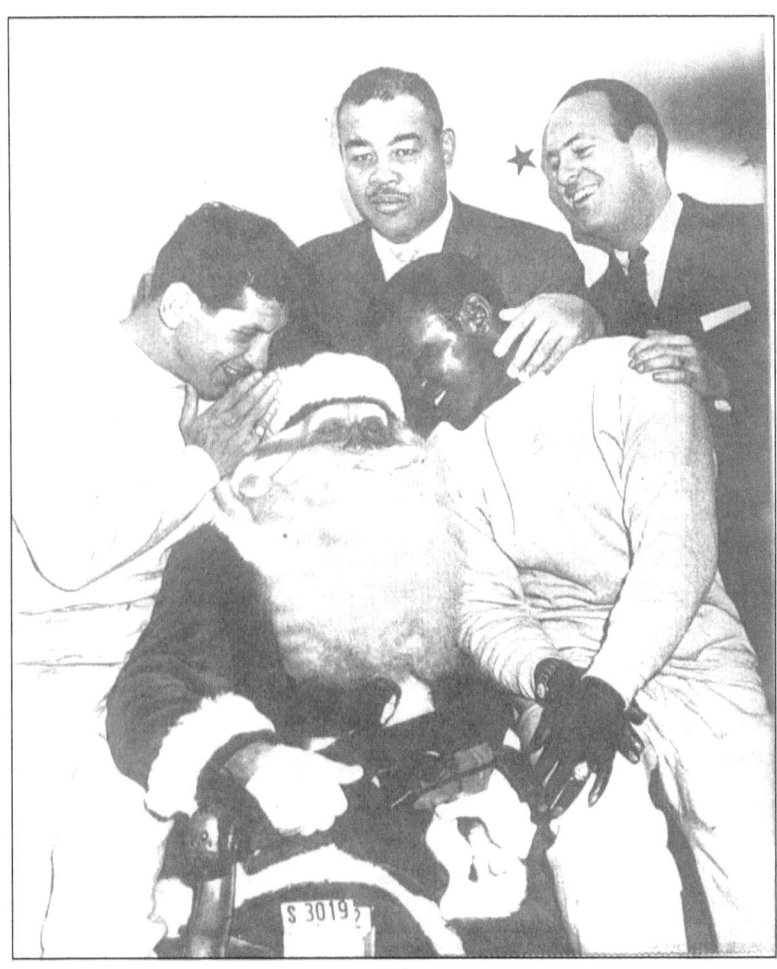

A novelty Christmas publicity shot arranged to promote their upcoming World Middleweight Title fight; Champion Dick Tiger and challenger Joey Giardello each make a request from Santa Claus. Former World Heavyweight Champion (1937-49) and boxing legend, Joe Louis standing in the middle behind the fighters closely observes the spectacle

Photographs

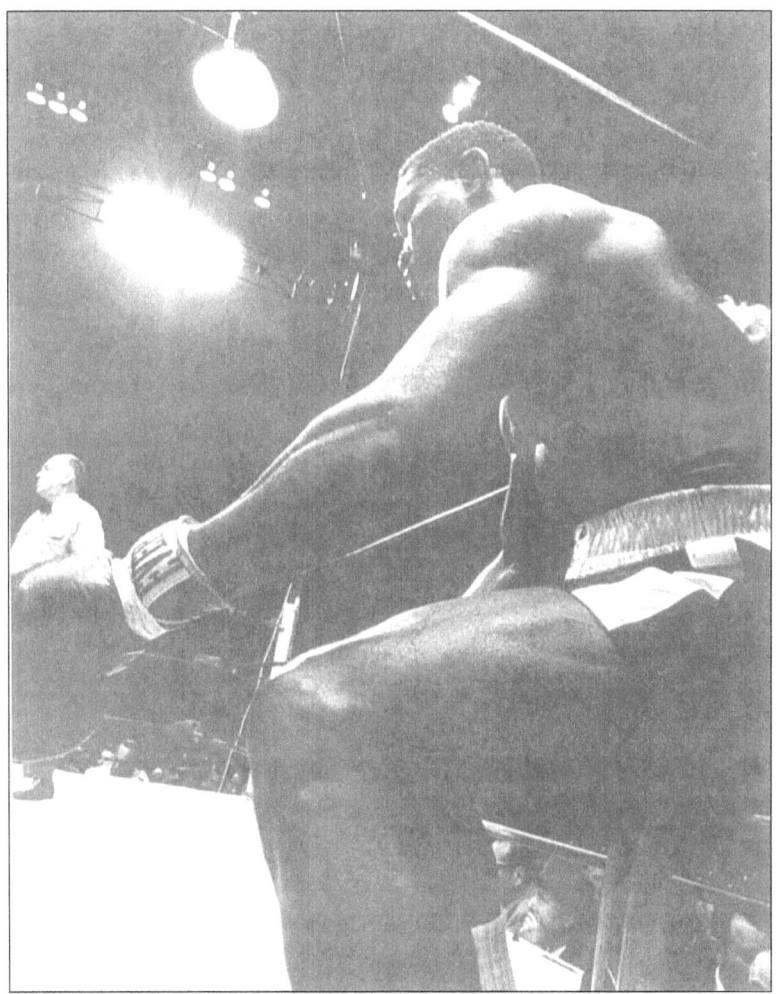

Tiger in between the rounds of one of his 81 or more ring battles, raring to go for the next round

A press shot from the intense no-holds-barred ring battle between Dick Tiger and Frank DePaula of October 1968, which featured four dramatic knockdowns and was voted "Fight of the Year" by *The Ring* Magazine

Photographs

The rising World Middleweight Contender cowers over a fallen Spider Webb after seventh round knockdown during their April 15, 1961 bout in New York City

Tiger connects with a wicked straight left to the jaw of Italian idol and reigning World Middleweight Champion, Nino Benvenutti en route to defeating the Italian in a non-title bout, May 1969

Photographs

Upon moving his base to the USA in 1959, Dick Tiger fought a couple of fights against American top contender, Rory Calhoun. Here Tiger fields a low blow from Calhoun in a middleweight bout held in New York City on June 5, which was ruled a draw by the judges. (Courtesy, *The Daily Times* of Nigeria)

Joey Giardello breaks through Tiger's defense to crack in a solid right cross to Tiger's chin in one of their action-filled encounters

Photographs

A pillar of society in his home region in Eastern Nigeria, Dick Tiger was much loved and respected by members of his Igbo ethnic group, and indeed also by all Nigerians, before the politics of the Nigerian Civil War estranged him from the Federal authorities. Here along with his wife, Abigail, Tiger is feted by leading Igbo chiefs including the self-declared "Political Juggernaut", Chief K. O. Mbadiwe at a traditional ceremony in Owerri. (Courtesy, *The Daily Times* of Nigeria).

Tiger and wife, Abigail wave goodbye to fans and friends while about to board a plane flight out of the Lagos International Airport circa 1965 (Courtesy, *The Daily Times* of Nigeria)

Photographs

Dick Tiger numbered many Nigerian dignitaries among his teeming fans in the country. One of such was the venerable Chief Simeon Adebo, Nigeria's first Ambassador to the United Nations seen here enthusiastically receiving an autograph from the World Champion circa 1965 (Courtesy *The Daily Times* of Nigeria)

There were several awards and honors bestowed on Dick Tiger while alive and also posthumously. However, this photo shows the presentation of free flight tickets to him and his wife by officials of the British Overseas Airways Corporation (BOAC) in Lagos in recognition of his frequent patronage of the airline on his regular trips abroad, circa 1966 (Courtesy, *The Daily Times* of Nigeria)

Dick Tiger who won the hearts of British fight fans while based in Liverpool England takes time out from training camp to sample the Scottish bag pipes (circa 1959)

Signing of the Dick Tiger-Jose Torres World Light Heavyweight title rematch of 1968: behind the Champion and the challenger are renowned British promoter, Jack Solomons and Dick Tiger's manager, Jersey Jones (Courtesy of *The Daily Times* of Nigeria)

Photographs

Tiger evades a straight left from Puerto Rico's Jose Torres and counterpunches with his own enroute to dethroning the World Light Heavyweight Champion, December 1966.

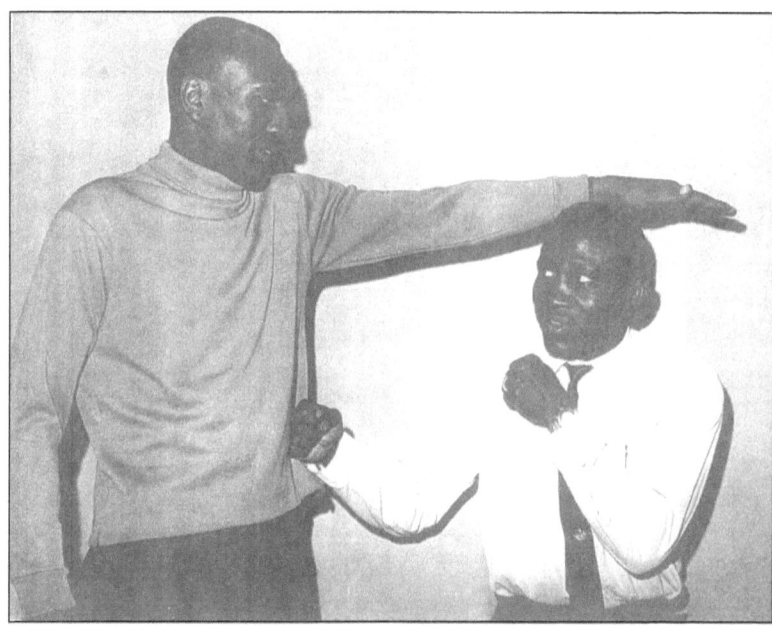

David and Goliath? The vast height and other disparities in physical attributes between 5ft 8in Light Heavyweight Champion, Dick Tiger and 6ft 3in Challenger, Bob Foster are put on display for the press prior to their May 1968 title bout in New York

Photographs

The popular World press photo that highlighted multiple world champion Richard Ihetu a.k.a. Dick Tiger (1929-71) at his fighting prime in 1967 — the world titles he won included the WBA Middleweight Championship (1962-63) Unified World Middleweight Championship (1963, 1965-66) and World Light Heavyweight Championship (1966-68)

Another popular press photo of the prime Tiger that circulated among the world's major sports news mediums of the mid-1960s.

Photographs

November 13, 1963 the undisputed World Middleweight Champion skips rope during training a month before his title defense against Joey Giardello

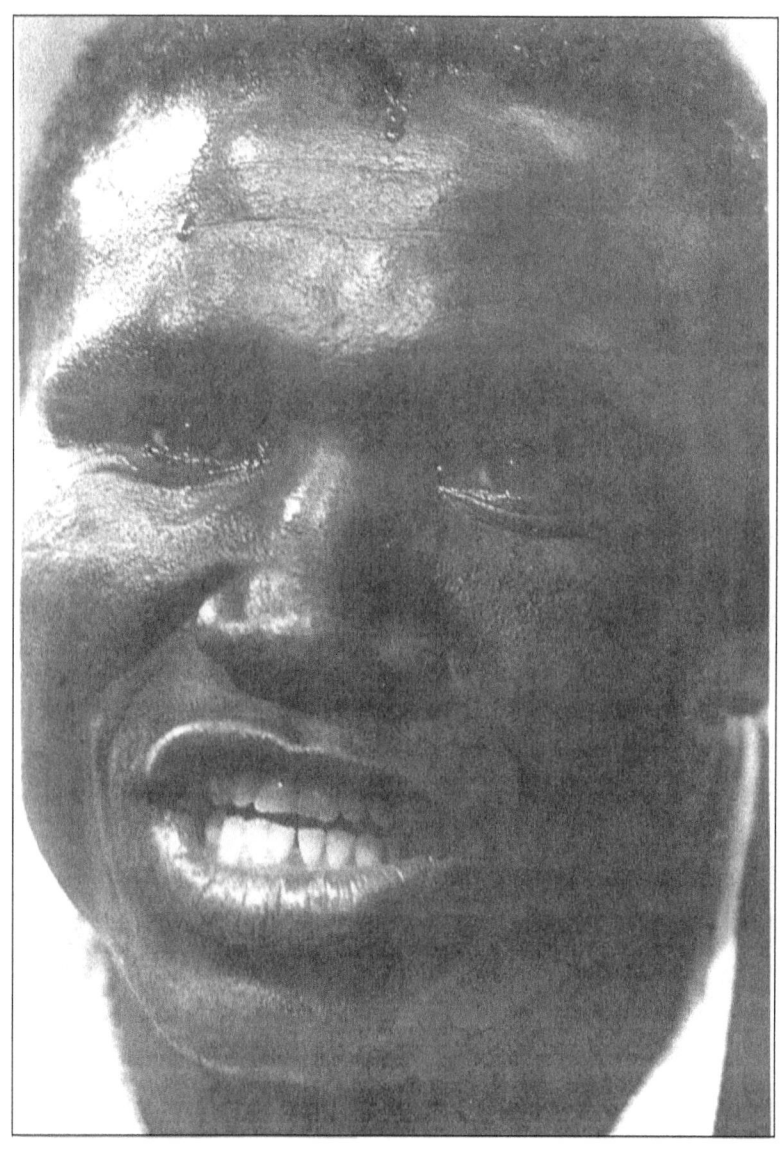

Dick Tiger the Pride of Africa!

Photographs

August 1971: Dick Tiger with three of his children at the International Airport in Lagos. The effects of his terminal illness seem apparent from his leanness. Four months later, the former multiple world champion died peacefully near his birthplace of Amaigbo-Orlu (Courtesy of *The Daily Times* of Nigeria)

The Tiger is laid to rest, December 1971: Amid grieving relatives, friends and general sympathizers the casket of Dick Tiger is carried to his final resting place. On the left-hand side of photo is his visibly grief-stricken wife, Abigail. (Courtesy *The Daily Times* of Nigeria)

Chapter Five

THE MULTIPLE WORLD CHAMPION AND THE NIGERIAN CIVIL WAR

On October 21, 1965, Dick Tiger regained the undisputed world middleweight title from Joey Giardello at Madison Square Garden, New York City. After a grueling 15-round title bout, the former titleholder was reinstated champion. He had delivered the more effective body punching during the encounter, hurting Giardello consistently throughout. Tiger thus secured the approval of the judges on the scorecards and began a second reign as the world's middleweight champion. For successfully reclaiming the undisputed title, both *The Ring* Magazine and the Boxing Writers Association of America (BWAA) again honored the Nigerian boxer by declaring him "Fighter of the Year" for 1965.

In Tiger's Nigerian homeland however, the national euphoria that had greeted his previous international ring victories was ebbing away as the political situation in the country had begun to change dramatically. Local developments in the African nation were now heading on ominously towards a bloody three-year civil war during which millions of Nigerians, the majority of whom were Tiger's Igbo kinsmen, would die from the violence of warfare as well as from famine and mass starvation.

The war would invariably have a profoundly adverse effect on the champion's personal life because of the strong roots he had maintained over the years in his birthplace of Amaigbo, deep in the theater of the coming warfare. While he had been abroad, first in England and later in the US, where he had campaigned professionally for the most part of the years from 1955, Tiger had regularly returned home to be with his family and kinsmen as often as his fight regimen would allow. Abigail, his wife had by now had their eight children and the responsibility of seeing to the welfare and upbringing of the young Ihetus was the pre-eminent consideration of the champion.

Wisely keeping in view that his boxing career would one day come to an end, Tiger had undertaken various business initiatives in the country to ensure that he was able to provide a good future for his family after he would have retired from the boxing ring. Drawing from his people's well-known flair for commercial astuteness and his early experience in trading in Aba, the world champion turned out a shrewd entrepreneur, investing a sizeable proportion of his ring earnings profitably in real estate in the rapidly urbanizing Nigerian capital city of Lagos and also in areas of his home region in the country's Eastern Region. The returns on these successful investments enabled him to see to the general upkeep of his extended family, including distant relations and his community at large. He founded a secondary school in his hometown and also established trust funds to guarantee the education of his children, while providing them all with a stable family life and decent living conditions. However, the coming social upheaval

The Multiple World Champion and the Nigerian Civil War

in Nigeria in general and the particular targets of violence which the Igbo ethnic group was to become, could only portend an ill wind for the world champion.

With the arrival of the new year in 1966, the political cleavage in Nigeria deepened perilously. In mid-January, junior military officers led by Major Chukwuma Kaduna Nzeogwu attempted to overthrow the civilian government in a bloody coup d'etat. Although senior officers were able to suppress the young Turks, and end their bloody rebellion, the die had been cast and Nigeria's First Republic had been effectively truncated. The key functionaries of the civilian administration, which had been inaugurated at independence, including the Prime Minister, Sir Abubakar Tafawa Balewa had been brutally assassinated, inflicting a deep wound on the collective psyche of a segment of the country. For this, the aggrieved would seek and enact vengeance against their perceived adversaries in short order, leading to a spiral of violence that would very nearly consume the whole country and split apart its constituent ethnic groups.

For the reinstated world middleweight champion however, the beginning of 1966 was business as usual. In February he traveled to Dortmund, Germany to engage German contender, Peter Mueller in a non-title bout. Despite the advantage of fighting on his home turf, Mueller was given a thorough trouncing and eventually knocked out by Tiger in the third round. Next in line for the middleweight champion was the consummate fighter from the Virgin Islands, Emile Griffith. Griffith was a three-time world welterweight champion seeking to add the middleweight crown to his laurels. He was nearly a decade younger than Tiger who by now was approaching his thirty seventh birthday.

Tiger defended against Griffith on April 25, 1966, in the New York Madison Square Garden. The middleweight champion faced a stern challenge from the welterweight champion turned middleweight challenger who fought brilliantly, combining speed with determination. The Virgin Islander stealthily evaded most of tiger's punches and outboxed the Nigerian over the scheduled fifteen rounds. Griffith, a future member of the International Boxing Hall of Fame, thus secured the judges' decision in his favor by a comfortable margin and again the Tiger was shorn of his middleweight crown. Barely six months after regaining the world title, he had lost it in the very first defense of his second reign! Aged nearly 37, it seemed to most observers at the time, that the best of the boxing career of the Nigerian dynamo was now behind him. However, Dick Tiger would yet again confound the skeptics. In his very next fight and before the end of the year, he moved up in weight and dethroned the world light heavyweight champion, Jose Torres.

Before Tiger's ascension to the pinnacle of boxing's light heavyweight division however, the deteriorating political situation in his Nigerian homeland was to gain an even more dangerous momentum. The bloody military coup of January had been planned and executed by mainly officers of Tiger's Igbo ethnic group of the Eastern Region, which was predominantly Christian. On the other hand, majority of the key members of the civilian government who were assassinated were Moslems from the Northern Region. Apart from the aforementioned Prime Minister Tafawa Balewa, the murder victims included Sir Ahmadu Bello, (the powerful and highly respected premier of the Northern Region who was a major spiritual leader of Nigerian Moslems) and various other northern leaders, both civilian politicians and military officers.

The Multiple World Champion and the Nigerian Civil War

Even if the January conspirators had had genuinely noble goals of redeeming the country from the corrupt rule of politicians as they claimed, the one-sided appearance of the ethnic and religious affiliations of their victims painted the coup as a sectional one directed against the Moslem north. Incidentally, the most senior ranking officer, Major General J. T. U. Aguiyi-Ironsi, who rallied loyal forces to quell the mutiny and who thereafter assumed power fortuitously from the remnants of the decimated civilian leadership, was himself of Igbo ancestry. His indecisiveness in bringing the January conspirators to trial, despite having detained them, further heightened the suspicions of the northerners. In May 1966, Ironsi abolished the country's federal structure in apparent disregard of northern sensitivities and established a unitary state. This act further exacerbated northern fears and suspicions, convincing the majority that there was a sinister conspiracy by the Igbo ethnic group to subjugate northern ethnic groups, primarily the Hausa and other sub-nationalities in the country under Igbo domination. Rather than serving to arrest the corrupt rule of the civilian administration as professed by the January 1966 coup plotters, their insurrection was about to lead to an escalation of the chain of domestic violence in the country that had begun after an election crisis in the Western Region in 1964. This chain of violence would ultimately evolve into violent riots and pogroms culminating finally into a fullblown civil war that would hold the whole world in awe for three long years!

On July 29, 1966, a counter coup was launched by northern elements within the Nigerian army in reprisal against the Igbo and to restore political power to the north. General Ironsi and other leading members of his government from the Eastern and Western Regions of the country were brutally murdered including the military governor of the Western Region, Lieutenant Colonel Adekunle Fajuyi. A number of the January conspirators that were detained in areas within the reach of the perpetrators of the counter coup were also spirited out of their cells, tortured and killed. In the weeks and months that followed, there were indiscriminate attacks by northerners against ordinary Igbo men and women who had settled in areas of the country outside their home region in the east. It all but seemed that the country was about to fall apart with each of the three regions going its separate way. However, Britain and other Western nations as well as the international community at large prevailed on the emergent northern-dominated government not to allow the Nigerian federation to break up, pointing out that it was in the government's best interest to keep the country together. Nonetheless, various efforts at national reconciliation failed to bring about a peaceful resolution of the Nigerian crisis. The animosities continued unabated, with the Igbo suffering the brunt of the destruction and looting of assets and properties that flared up in the Northern and Western Regions of the country. The Igbos in retaliation attacked northerners domiciled in the Eastern Region, though this counter-reaction was nowhere as close in magnitude to the sufferings the Igbos experienced in the Northern Region and other non-Igbo areas.

It was under these circumstances of anxiety and tension in his Nigerian homeland that Dick Tiger secured a challenge for the undisputed world light heavyweight title held by Puerto Rico's Jose Torres in December 1966. Tiger surrendered eight pounds to the champion, who also held the advantage of youth, being the younger man by nearly seven years. Unsurprisingly therefore, the Nigerian went into the fight a three-to- one betting underdog, with most of the bookmakers and observers expecting that he would be easily defeated by the Puerto Rican world title holder. However, over the course of the 15-round championship bout at the New York Madison Square Garden, Tiger fought far more aggressively and effectively than the champion. The former world middleweight champion won a close but unanimous decision thereby becoming a two-division world champion, a feat no other African boxer had accomplished up till this time, thereby establishing himself as the continent's most internationally accomplished fighter in the modern era of the sport.

Early in 1967, Dick Tiger was back in his beleaguered homeland as the Nigerian political situation oscillated between reconciliation efforts and continued violent ethnic clashes, the major brunt of which was still being suffered by his Igbo kinsmen. Adding further fuel to the explosive equation was a personality clash between the leaders on both sides of the confrontation, coupled with their uncompromising positions towards solving the crisis. This deadlock blocked the prospects of various peace moves initiated from both within the country and abroad. Colonel Yakubu Gowon later promoted major general, a member of a northern minority ethnic group had emerged head of state after the assassination of General Ironsi. Acting at the behest of his northern constituents, Gowon called for a federal structure for the country with a relatively strong center, which the regional governments were to defer to on all major issues. On the other hand, Colonel Emeka Odumegwu-Ojukwu, military governor of the Eastern Region who had therefrom emerged as the leader of the Igbos, demanded for a loose confederation, which would allow the regions considerable autonomy including the right of secession. Furthermore, Ojukwu refused to accept the authority of Gowon as head of state arguing that Gowon was not the most senior ranking officer and thus had no right to succeed the assassinated Ironsi as head of state.

As the crisis deepened and the controversy over the country's leadership raged on between Gowon and Ojukwu, the random attacks against the Igbo in the Northern and Western Regions continued uncontrolled. Shortly, a mass exodus of the Igbo began, with hundreds of thousands of its nine million members who had been domiciled in other parts of the country fleeing back to their hometowns in the Eastern Region for safety. Conversely, non-easterners domiciled in the Eastern Region began to leave for their own home areas, with the military governor declaring that their safety could no longer be guaranteed by the regional government.

On February 5, 1967, Tiger fought a non-title bout in his troubled homeland. Barring the world title fight against Fullmer in 1963, this was the first time in twelve years that Tiger would fight in Nigeria since 1955 when he left the country's shores for Liverpool, England. His opponent, fellow Nigerian, Abraham Tonica was a well-respected boxer who had won national laurels of his own. The fight was held in the eastern coastal city of Port Harcourt that would soon become a part of the theater of the impending war. Tiger came into the fight with a record of 55 wins, 15 losses and three draws (with 25 knock outs) according to the IBHOF records. The world light heavyweight champion defeated Tonica in the non-title bout by a ten round decision.

On May 30, 1967, reacting to the abrogation of the country's regional framework and the creation of a twelve-state federal structure for Nigeria by Nigeria's federal government, the military government of the Eastern Region formally declared secession from the Nigerian federation and proclaimed the

Eastern Region, the independent Republic of Biafra. That same month Tiger who had returned to his fight base in the US defended his title against the former title-holder Jose Torres in New York. The result of the rematch was same as the first fight, with Tiger awarded a 15-round decision for his greater work rate and more effective aggression against the Puerto Rican.

Unfortunately, the decision in Tiger's favor was unpopular to the largely Hispanic fans at the fight venue, precipitating a near-riot. Chairs, broken bottles and other dangerous objects and implements were tossed into the ring and around the arena by the irate Hispanic fans, targeted at the champion and members of the officiating authorities. The affable and good-natured champion took the situation in his stride and would not let the unreasonable mob action bother him. To his own credit, Torres accepted the decision graciously and expressed no ill feelings against his two time conqueror.

By the end of June 1967, formal warfare had finally broken out in Nigeria with the federal forces poised against the secessionist Biafran army. Dick Tiger, once regarded as a symbol of Nigeria's national pride and the country's frontline international sports hero, was faced with the moral dilemma of deciding what position to take on the warfare. There were three potential options open to him. The safest was for him to maintain neutrality and not get personally involved in the war. He could easily have evacuated his family from the war zone and have them join him abroad, safely away from the violence and destruction unfolding in their home region. With his international standing, getting the right of domicile for himself and his loved ones in the US or England would have been merely a formality for the world champion.

The two other options open to Tiger were much more difficult. He could have chosen to turn his back on the rebellion of his kinsmen and pledge his support to the federal side as some of his fellow Igbo kinsmen did. Alternatively, he could join in the rebellion and technically become a traitor to the Nigerian government. There were no compelling reasons to make him take the harder decisions. He was never a professional soldier and although he was a national figure, he had never shown a proclivity for partisan politics. Naturally, the two opposing forces realized the public relations' value of having an internationally renowned sports figure and the world's light heavyweight champion on its side and Tiger was wooed by both. Of these two alternatives however, the less risky for Tiger would have been to pitch his support for the more powerful Federal side, which had the backing of Britain and other world powers and was clearly in the better position to win the war.

Characteristic of Tiger, the considerations over what stand he ought to take on the Nigerian crisis transcended merely opting for the safest or easier alternatives. His life had been an epitome of struggle against tremendous odds. Already he had far exceeded the life expectations of an individual born dirt-poor in the rural backwoods of Nigeria with little opportunities open to him. Yet, after he pondered over the situation, he was ready to risk all he had achieved to stand by his kinsmen in what they considered rightly or wrongly as a battle for their collective survival. He chose not to settle for the narrow interest of looking out for only himself and his immediate family, or pitching his tent with the stronger faction more likely to win the war. Against the odds, he decided to stand by his Igbo kinsmen and be counted among his kith and kin in the life and death struggle that was unfolding.

The Multiple World Champion and the Nigerian Civil War

Expectedly, Tiger's decision to support the Biafran rebellion was seriously opposed by many of his Nigerian friends. Among them was his old mentor, Chief Ganiyu Kolawole Balogun, who had assisted Tiger in the early stages of his fight career in the 1950s and who had also been an ardent supporter of the fighter over the years as his career progressed. Balogun, a member of the Yoruba ethnic group from the Western Region and a supporter of the federalist cause at the time of the outbreak of hostilities, claimed to have advised Tiger against associating himself with the secessionist campaign, pointing out the futility of the struggle and the ominous prospects that Tiger's direct involvement in the war effort portended for his career. So charged were the emotions of the time that even nearly three decades after the end of the war, when Balogun was interviewed by this author for *The Ring* Magazine's tribute to mark the twenty-fifth anniversary of Tiger's death in January 1997, the Nigerian sports enthusiast still showed indignation over the matter. According to him: "Tiger ruined himself." "Had he been wiser and not involved himself in the futile parochial cause, his life story would most certainly have been more glorious."

However, Tiger was driven by a much higher ideal than that of mere self-survival or self-preservation. While in Nigeria he had witnessed first-hand, the physical destruction and carnage wreaked on Owerri, one of the several towns and villages of his home region, where bombs were dropped indiscriminately by Nigerian Air Force fighter jets, flown mainly by mercenary pilots from Europe. He was also aware of the thousands of innocent men, women, and young children of his ethnic group, some of whom were his relatives and personal friends, who had suffered the terrible consequences of the massacres that presaged the war and the many more whose lives were sacrificed as the war began to rage in earnest. The world champion thus considered it only honorable and conscientious to enlist in the Biafran Army and to join his kinsmen in their collective struggle against Nigeria's federal forces. A true loyalist to the Igbo people that spawned him, he put their collective welfare first, above his self-interest at great personal risk to himself and his family.

Before making his decision public however, Dick Tiger made a final successful defense of his light heavyweight title in Las Vegas, Nevada on November 17, 1967. His challenger, American top-ten contender, Roger Rouse put up a brave effort in the attempt to wrest the title from the champion. However, Tiger knocked out Rouse sensationally in the twelfth round, prompting *The Ring* Magazine to declare this as the "Round of the Year" for 1967. Two months later, Tiger announced to the world press that he had enlisted in the Biafran army. He proudly displayed his olive-green military uniform with its lieutenant's epaulette and the Biafran rising sun shoulder band to the *New York Times'* Lloyd Garrison, who visited him in the Biafran stronghold of Port Harcourt in late 1967. The champion stated candidly to the veteran journalist that just as he had never been afraid to fight any challenger in the boxing ring, he was not afraid to fight for "his people".

Notwithstanding his readiness to join in the actual physical combat of the army, Dick Tiger's role in the Biafran campaign was naturally more valued for its symbolic nature and the morale booster it could provide the Biafran troops on the field and the civilian population at home. As Africa's most outstanding contemporary boxer, he was better placed serving as an international public relations functionary for the Biafran

The Multiple World Champion and the Nigerian Civil War

cause, rather than as an easily expendable foot soldier. In recognition of this fact, the Biafran army did not have him posted to the war front and engaged him mainly for its public relations campaigns. He also contributed substantially to the Biafran war effort in financial terms, donating regularly to the cause from his personal earnings and engaging in fund raising campaigns abroad. In addition, he acted as an unofficial ambassador overseas, seeking support from the outside world for his people's struggle. Nonetheless, Tiger's potential as an image-enhancing asset and morale booster for the Biafran troops was never fully realized by the Biafran high command, which was poorly led and also bedeviled by internal intrigues. Through all this, the world champion continued his boxing career, even though with much less drive than hitherto for the obvious reasons of the great distraction the involvement in the war constituted.

In May 1968, Tiger, now nearing his thirty-ninth year, defended his title against Bob Foster. The American top-contender had distinguished himself in the light heavyweight division and earned the title-shot by racking up seven straight wins over other top contenders of the division in 1967, six by knock outs. Foster held virtually all the physical advantages; he was the younger man by almost a decade, at six feet three inches, he enjoyed a seven-inch height advantage over Tiger, in addition to a seven and a half inch advantage in reach. The bookmakers thus installed the American a 12-5 favorite over the Nigerian world champion prior to the fight.

On May 24, 1967, 11,547 fight fans showed up at the New York Madison Square Garden to watch the championship fight. The champion was formally introduced as being from the "Republic of Biafra" and described as a "lieutenant in the Biafran army", in deference to his request to be identified with his kinsmen's struggle, and notwithstanding the fact that the US never officially granted recognition to the rebellious breakaway republic like a few countries did. At any rate the champion acquitted himself laudably in the early going, clearly rattling Foster with a double-fisted body attack in the first round. The blow by blow analyst calling the fight on the television broadcast even acknowledged the champion may have done enough to win the first two rounds. However, the American challenger seized control as from the third round, utilizing his considerable height and reach advantages to bombard Tiger with jarring long-range jabs. Just aabout the first minute of the fourth round, Foster connected with a chopping right uppercut followed by a devastating left hook that landed flush on Tiger's chin, sending the champion to the canvass for a knockout defeat. He was counted out in one minute and five seconds of the round. This was only the second knockout loss Tiger would ever suffer in his eighteen year, 81-bout career. The sensational sequence ending the fight in the fourth round earned *The Ring* Magazine's honor as "Round of the Year" for 1968.

Tiger was as humble in defeat as he had always been gracious in victory. He congratulated the newly crowned champion and gave credit to him for his victorious performance, while wishing him well during his championship reign. However, characteristic of the consummate and unrelenting fighter he was, the dethroned champion also put his conqueror on notice that he would fight on and expect to secure the opportunity of reclaiming the title in due course.

Chapter Six

A FULL CIRCLE

As the Nigerian Civil War raged on between 1968 and 1969, Dick Tiger continued to fight professionally in the US while making considerable financial contributions to the war effort of his "Biafran" kinsmen from his ring earnings. He shuttled between his war-torn homeland and the Western world, flying circuitous air routes to evade Nigerian authorities and the federal operatives seeking to eliminate him. When the situation in the areas within the war zone grew particularly dangerous with Nigeria's federal forces having overrun most of the Biafran enclave, he decided to move Abigail and the young children to a safe haven. Late in 1968 he found one in Portugal, where he evacuated the family to and from where they were to later join him in the United States.

Though he would never again engage in a world title fight, Tiger still had a good number of significant victories to notch up on his professional record before retiring from the ring. In October 1968, five months after losing the light heavyweight title to Foster, the ex-champion took on Frank DePaula at the New York Madison Square Garden. The light heavyweight bout was memorable for the frenzy the two combatants whipped the watching crowd into by the intensity and sheer brutality of their encounter. Going into the fifth round, each fighter had scored two dramatic knockdowns against the other. Thereafter Tiger roared ahead and ultimately outpointed DePaula over the last five equally thrilling rounds of the fight. Tiger had again confounded the skeptics who assumed that at the advanced age of 39, he could no longer perform at the top of his game. And once again *The Ring* Magazine honored Tiger by designating the action-packed duel against DePaula "Fight of the Year" for 1968.

Tiger's next opponent was Nino Benvenuti, the Italian idol who along with the legendary Muhammad Ali, had won Olympic stardom in Rome at the 1960 games and then gone on to begin a successful professional boxing career the following year. Benvenuti had held the junior middleweight title from 1965 to 1966 and also won, lost and regained the middleweight title from Tiger's successor, Emile Griffith, between 1967 and 1968. The Italian's world middleweight title was however, not at stake when he fought against Dick Tiger at the Madison Square Garden in May of 1969. Had it been, the Nigerian would have emerged as a three-time middleweight titlist as he defeated the Italian idol in the non-title bout.

The situation on Nigeria's warfront was in the meantime approaching a climax. As the end of 1969 approached, Nigerian federal forces had gained considerable ground against the secessionist Biafrans, with much of the Biafran territory having fallen under federal control. It was becoming apparent that the Nigerian Civil War would soon be over, and that it was only a matter of time before the rebels would be completely overrun. In protest against Britain's support of the federal forces, Tiger returned to the British embassy in Washington DC the medal presented to him in 1963 to commemorate his admission to the Order of the British Empire (OBE).

Phil Pepe of the *New York Daily News* who interviewed Tiger at the time, later quoted the fighter's *raison d'être* for his actions in an article published in December 1971. He couldn't keep the medal, Tiger had said, "because every time I look at it, I think of the millions of men, women and children who are dying" in the Nigerian Civil War. Such were the strong emotions and the compassion that the fighter had for his people. And yet when the Biafran secessionist campaign would eventually collapse and some of its leaders would flee into exile, the fighter who had pitched his unconditional support for his kinsmen, and who lost so much in the process, would accept the situation eschewing all bitterness.

Two months before the official armistice ending the Nigerian Civil War, in November 1969, Dick Tiger won a 10-round bout against American light heavyweight top-ten contender, Andy Kendall in New York. For this victory the fighter from Amaigbo gained recognition as the world's leading contender for the light heavyweight world title now held by Bob Foster. But before he could secure a rematch against Foster, Tiger attempted to avenge his other major loss to Virgin Islander, Emile Griffith. A rematch between the two former world middleweight champions was set for July 15, 1970, at the Madison Square Garden, a venue both men had come to be well acquainted with in the last couple of years. This officially would be the final professional bout of the Nigerian three-time world champion.

The Biafran struggle had become a lost cause by the time of the second Tiger-Griffith bout. Before the end of 1969, the rebel forces had been completely routed by Nigeria's federal troops. With his domain having virtually shrunk to nothing, Biafran military leader, Emeka Odumegwu-Ojukwu fled from the war zone to the West African country of Ivory Coast in early 1970. He left behind a tape of his voice for broadcast on Biafra radio, still extolling rebel troops to fight to the last man!

Many of the Igbo who survived the bloody three-year war, invariably found that they had lost virtually all their earthly possessions. Prominent among these unfortunate souls was Dick Tiger. Most of his real estate investments in Lagos, estimated by him at $103,000 at the time had either been confiscated or requisitioned by the federal military government. Regardless of the monumental material losses he had suffered however, the former world champion never showed any bitterness, anger or regret, neither did he expect sympathy from any quarters. Just before the final Griffith fight, he acknowledged quite candidly to the *New York Times* that the war had been lost. "Now that the war is over", he said, "I am from Nigeria again. After this fight I hope to go home again to see my family."

Unfortunately for Dick Tiger, there would be no grand finale to his long and distinguished boxing career. Griffith defeated him by a close decision in the rematch of July 1970. At age 40, going on 41, his once considerable fighting skills were clearly in erosion. It was also apparent that he no longer commanded the drawing power to secure for him continued lucrative fights worth the risks involved in his potentially fatal sport of fist fighting. Fully aware of these realities, Dick Tiger announced his retirement from boxing in early 1971. He had decided that he would not allow himself to be relegated into a trial horse for up-and-coming young fighters like so many former champions of the past. Even if there would not be a glorious ending to his 18-year romance with the fight game, he would at least bow

A Full Circle

out honorably and avoid an embarrassing exit that could have overshadowed his great ring achievements over the years.

Following his retirement, Tiger was faced with the hard realities of having lost much of his life savings and financial investments in Nigeria. He however was far from having been made indigent or broke as many sources erroneously assumed. He was able to retain or regain a few of his physical assets in Nigeria including a housing estate in a major commercial area of the country's capital city of Lagos, and other landed properties in Port Harcourt and in areas around his hometown in Owerri. These physical assets, in addition to the education trust funds he had put in place for his children, guaranteed the family's continued well-being and decent living.

It was therefore not in desperation, as some have averred, that Tiger chose to work after his retirement from boxing as a security guard at the New York Metropolitan Museum of Art. Clearly, he needed a steady income and considered that his vast experience in a physical vocation qualified him as suitable for such work. Unlike most men who may have enjoyed the material success he had in the past, Tiger's humble and sober nature precluded him from considering this as beneath him or humiliating in any way. To him, it was just a practical means of earning an income pending when he was ready to return to his homeland finally. However, it should be noted that the retired multiple world champion had traveled a full-circle in life, recalling that he had worked as a night guard in Ibadan, Nigeria several years before, at the beginning of his fight career in the early 1950s.

In July 1971, Tiger was hospitalized in New York City, having suddenly fallen ill. After a careful examination of his condition, his doctors discovered that he was terminally ill, suffering from the late symptoms of cancer of the liver and their prognosis gave him only a few months left to live. The fighter who had refused to forsake his people in their time of need, and who had valiantly contributed his full measure to their failed struggle, decided to prepare to return home to die among his beloved kinsmen. Following official assurances from the Nigerian government of his safe passage, reportedly witnessed by the world-renowned boxing journalist Larry Merchant, Tiger returned home shortly after the diagnosis. On December 14, 1971 Richard Ihetu aka Dick Tiger died peacefully in Aba, near his birthplace of Amaigbo. He passed on in the loving care of his dear wife, Abigail and close relations who had rallied round to be with him as he succumbed to the terminal illness he was afflicted with. Within a week of his death the deceased champion was buried in his birthplace. During the emotion-laden funeral ceremony, an estimated 20,000 people including his kinsmen, relations, fans and general sympathizers, lined the dusty roadsides to Amaigbo to view the funeral procession arriving from Aba and pay their last respects to their fallen hero. Following a 21-gun salute, Richard Ihetu aged 42, three-time world boxing champion, and a great, even though controversial African patriot was finally laid to rest.

Epilogue

THE LEGACY OF AFRICA'S MOST ACCOMPLISHED BOXER

After Dick Tiger's death, it was not surprising that Nigeria's military government did not consider it fit to send the Ihetu family any official message of condolence or commiserations due to his partisan role in the Biafran rebellion. However, heartrending tributes came pouring in for the family from all over the world. Obituaries and words of homage appeared in various international papers including the *New York Times*, *The London Times* and numerous other international news mediums and boxing journals.

On December 17, 1971, a tepid official announcement of Dick Tiger's death was made by the Nigerian embassy in Washington DC. The following day a report of the passing of the former world champion was published in the *New York Times* written by Dave Anderson. According to the journalist, the fighter's American manager, Willis "Jersey" Jones had estimated Tiger's total earnings in his eighteen- year career at half a million dollars. This was by no means a meager sum for boxers by the general standards of the day. In fact, at the time, it was a most handsome, if not stupendous fortune in Tiger's Nigerian homeland. In the ensuing years during which Nigeria's national currency underwent a double digit devaluation, this estimation of Tiger's total earnings would be regarded as a colossal fortune in the country. The magnitude of his material losses as a result of the Nigerian Civil War can best be imagined under this light.

However, the legacy of Dick Tiger far transcended the purses or material gains he made from his fight career. It was also much more than his impressive championship record, even though this is still arguably, unsurpassed by any other African pugilist over a half century after his retirement and transition to eternity. Rather, Tiger's legacy is more clearly manifest in his selflessness and the fact that he readily gave up much of his fortune over his principled stand at a time of grave national crisis in his homeland. As aforementioned, the fighter could easily have evaded any direct involvement in the ill-fated Biafran campaign and thereby avoided the eventual unfavorable outcome that befell him therefrom. Yet after the war, he did not express any regrets over his decision, neither did he complain about the loss of a good part of his wealth. He accepted the situation like a true stoic and never looked back with regret. Yet, very few of his kinsmen lost as much as Tiger did, for apart from much of his assets that he forfeited, he was also denied his rightful place in the sporting history of the country.

The legacy of Dick Tiger was one of a principled individual and a devoted member of his community, who stood above selfish material interests at all times during his abbreviated but well-fulfilled life. In addition, he should also be seen as a quintessential example of the good family man who did his very best for his wife and children. Throughout his sojourn

Epilogue: The Legacy of Africa's Most Accomplished Boxer

abroad in England and the USA during his fighting years, he always kept his family well provided for and sent money and gifts home to them regularly. And before his passing, He made sure he had put in place the mechanisms to guarantee their continued welfare and the education of his children, thereby ensuring a good future for them all.

The death of such a loving husband and father was traumatic for the prematurely widowed Abigail and the children and this led to hard times for them all, as they had to endure the untimely passage of their breadwinner and the loss of most of his earnings. However, the children were able to overcome their grief and forge better lives for themselves as they grew into adulthood. This was made possible by Abigail's own great efforts at rising to the occasion of having to play the dual role of both father and mother after the death of Tiger. She ensured that the trust funds instituted by her husband for the children's education and the remainder of his physical assets were well managed. She was thus able to maintain the decent standards of living of the family and she made sure that all of the eight children were educated right up to the highest levels of their abilities. On their own part the Ihetu children all worked very hard at their various educational pursuits, exhibiting the same dedication to work as their progenitor. The champion's first son, Richard, Jr. studied law and at the time the original edition of this biography was published in 2002 was running a reputable legal practice in their Nigerian homeland while all the other siblings had embarked on successful careers in other professional fields both within Nigeria and abroad. Among them, Justina was a high school teacher in New York City and Charles, an information technology specialist in Atlanta.

It is also instructive and thus worthy of mention that Dick Tiger chose to repatriate much of his considerable earnings to his homeland for investment rather than investing abroad in either of his two overseas bases or frittering away these earnings on living exorbitantly. It is well known that even as his incomes grew while abroad, he continued to live very frugally, eschewing the ostentatious and exuberant life-styles characteristic of most sports celebrities and so-called "super stars". Doubtlessly, Dick Tiger was of a rare breed, both very humble and self-effacing, despite his considerable fame and fortune.

As aforementioned, Tiger's death went virtually ignored by the Nigerian authorities, just as his great accomplishments have never been adequately acknowledged. However, members of the international boxing community showered the departed fighter with glowing tributes. Practically all those who had known him personally during his long career abroad had nothing but praises for the man from Amaigbo. Teddy Brenner, long-serving matchmaker at Madison Square Garden, who was responsible for pairing Tiger against several of his opponents, was among the well-known members of the international boxing fraternity who honored the memory of the departed champion.

"Tiger could have held his own against any fighter, in any era" Brenner stated, comparing the Nigerian with the great middleweight champions of the past including the legendary Sugar Ray Robinson, Jake Lamotta, Mickey Walker and Harry Greb. Harry Markson, Director of Boxing at the Madison Square Garden at the time, also noted, "Dick Tiger was a sweet, warm gentleman outside the ring". He further observed that though "Tiger was a tough businessman, ..once he made a deal,

Epilogue: The Legacy of Africa's Most Accomplished Boxer

you could sleep on it". Gene Fullmer, who could easily have harbored sour grapes against Tiger for having lost two world championship bouts against the Nigerian, called him "a great competitor and champion and, most importantly, a gentleman."

In the encyclopedic *Pictorial History of Boxing,* the late founder of *The Ring* Magazine and one of the most respected authorities on the sport, Nat Fleischer, described Tiger as "one of boxing's best liked heroes". Fleischer portrayed the Nigerian as "sincere, modest, affable and gentlemanly... a man of conscience." Even Tiger's old mentor, Chief Ganiyu Kolawole Balogun, who had severed relations with the boxer during the war and never again saw him thereafter, expressed nothing but respect for the champion on the twenty-fifth anniversary of his death. "No matter our differences" the Nigerian sports administrator and labor leader stated in late 1996, "I will always fly the Tiger's kite. He was a truly great fighter and a good and selfless man. His memory is one I will cherish till the day I die."

As noted in the acknowledgments pages, this writer had the opportunity of finally meeting with Mrs. Abigail Ihetu and her daughter, Justina in New York City at the concluding phase of the writing of this biography in mid-2001. After a very warm and amiable time interviewing the two, I wanted to know if there was any particular point they would like to convey to the readers for posterity. On behalf of her mother and herself, Justina commended the renewed efforts in Nigeria at forging national unity among the diverse groups within the federation and moving the country forward on the road to democracy following the recent end of a long military interregnum. She reiterated the fact that her father never had any regrets over the role he played during the civil war and neither did anyone in the family. However, she contended that if he were alive today, he would be "hundred percent Nigerian" and support and indeed promote the unity of the country. Going by her words, I concluded that just as Tiger's conscience had prompted him to stand by his kinsmen at the time of the outbreak of war, his honor had also made him rededicate himself to national unity once the hostilities were over.

As a three-time, two-division, undisputed world champion, Dick Tiger arguably won the pride of first place among African boxers of the modern era of the sport. His honesty, humility and decency also earned for him much respect and reverence from the boxing fraternity, which has endured over the years following his transition. In a professional sense, he has continued to be ranked highly in the annals of boxing history. Rating the world's forty middleweight champions between 1884 and 1980, in its June 1988 issue, *The Ring* Magazine placed Tiger sixth, behind only Sugar Ray Robinson, Argentina's Carlos Monzon, Stanley Ketchel, Emile Griffith and Harry Greb. Thirty four years later, in an updated "Ranking of *The Ring's* 31 Middleweight Champions" of all time, posted on its website in September 2022, Tiger was again ranked sixth, behind only Sugar Ray Robinson, Carlos Monzon, Marvin Hagler, Bernard Hopkins and Marcel Cerdan.

Tiger was inducted into the International Boxing Hall of Fame (I.B.H.O.F.) posthumously in 1991, the year after the establishment of the Hall at Canastota in New York State. He was the first and remained the only African boxer to be so honored until Ghana's Azumah Nelson was inducted in 2004. Tiger was also rated first on an all-time top ten list of African boxers in *The Ring* Magazine's issue of April 1996 compiled on behalf of the magazine by this author.

Epilogue: The Legacy of Africa's Most Accomplished Boxer

Indeed, boxing and aficionados of the fight game will never forget the man from Amaigbo, who rose from most humble origins to become champion of the world three times over. Without doubt, international honors and awards will continue rolling in for Tiger posthumously, for his remarkable boxing accomplishments and his humble and brave life. Perhaps what is left is for the Nigerian government and people to rehabilitate the image of this truly great son of Africa and world achieving prizefighter by establishing an enduring and befitting monument to his memory in his homeland. After all, the Nigerian Civil War is long over. In completing the healing process of the wounds inflicted on millions of innocent souls during the bloody encounter, Dick Tiger ought to be paid this due, which he so richly deserves.

AFTERWORD

The date was August 10, 1963. Very few of my generation, especially those who lived in Ibadan at that time, would forget that day or the controversies surrounding the Dick Tiger—Gene Fullmer boxing rematch. The excitement was high and everywhere. It was as if the world had descended on the ancient city of Ibadan. Even the gods were not left out, as rumor had it that they had been appeased to ensure that the weather remained favorable.

True or false, the rains came down only after Dick Tiger's victory, again, as if the gods wanted to participate in the celebration. It was a celebration not only for the victorious Tiger, but also for Nigeria as a nation, in her goal to register her imprints in the annals of international sports and live up to the hopes of a great and promising independent nation.

Dick Tiger: The Life and Times of Africa's Most Accomplished World Boxing Champion, is indeed a celebration of a true Nigerian hero. 'Damola Ifaturoti brings back to life both the boxing champion and the man in the champion, Richard Ihetu. The author has taken us from Tiger's humble beginnings, through his relentless and determined struggles to become world champion, and finally back to Amaigbo- Orlu, in Imo State, where the story began and rightly ends.

Afterword

Dick Tiger may have lacked the charm, charisma, and flair of Muhammad Ali, but his exploits and successes in the ring aroused and sustained our interest in boxing and perhaps prepared us for the coming of "The Greatest,"—Ali. Tiger was our worthy sports ambassador to the world.

His focus, determination and doggedness in the ring, and his gentleness, selflessness and humility outside the ring should stand as a shining model for present and future generations of sportsmen and women. His prizes and overall purse neither changed him, nor compelled him to abandon his principles. For this, he paid a price. Till the end, and in spite of the vicissitudes of life, he remained a responsible and caring husband and father.

Yet, the honor and glory he brought to his fatherland and to himself notwithstanding, Dick Tiger is hardly remembered today. This book should reverse that. Richard Ihetu (aka Dick Tiger) deserves our respect and honor for the respect and dignity he single-handedly brought to Nigeria at a time it was most needed. If ever his contributions were in doubt, this book Dick Tiger: The Life and Times of Africa's Most Accomplished World Boxing Champion should convince us.

Ifaturoti has done his share, and a worthy one too. It is now our turn and that of the nation Dick Tiger proudly showcased to the world.

Ambassador Joe Keshi
Consul-General of Nigeria, Atlanta, GA
September 17, 2001

APPENDIX 1

Author's article "25 Years After his Death Dick Tiger Remains a Champion" published in *The Ring* Magazine January 1997 issue

Appendix 1

The Best of the Best: "The best boxer of them all was Salvador Sanchez. He was in great condition, he was a great counterpuncher. He was quick. He was so smooth in the ring. Everything he did was smooth. He had it all. He was going to be a big, big star without that tragedy.

"As far as the guy who hit me the hardest, I don't even know. A few guys I fought were pretty good bangers. I'll tell you this: The fight that I felt it the most was against the kid, Kostya Tszyu. He hit me a shot to the body early, and I looked at Emile Griffith in my corner and said, 'Oh, s___.' I felt it when he hit me. He was strong. Very strong. I asked to fight him again when I was in better shape and they turned me down." ■

(Continued from page 33)

one of Tiger's mentors, recalls having facilitated the fighter's move to the Western Regional capital of Ibadan in 1954. Tiger worked as a night watchman at the nationally owned sports stadium to supplement his meager ring earnings. In 1955, Tiger moved to England, where he was given his fighting name. The British couldn't help but be impressed by the ferocity with which he mauled his opponents.

Early in his pro career, Tiger was victimized by several unfair decisions that may or may not have been the result of racism. At one point, he lost four consecutive fights on points. Nonetheless, he couldn't be denied for long, and in 1958, he won the British Empire middleweight title. By 1960, when Nigeria attained its independence from Britain, he had begun his rise to world-class status. Among his victims were Joey Giardello, Yolande Pompey, Holly Mims, Wilf Greaves, and Randy Sandy. But while Tiger gained international prominence and respect, the bold stand he made at a crucial crossroads in the political life of his country cost him dearly at home.

Tiger became a symbol of national pride for the new Nigerian nation in 1962, when, at age 33, he won the WBA middleweight title by outpointing Gene Fullmer in San Francisco. Even before the decision was announced, the Nigerians in attendance, including Hogan "Kid" Bassey, the nation's first world champion, lifted Tiger onto their shoulders in ring-center.

The 5'8" Tiger made his first defense in February 1963, keeping the title by 15-round draw against Fullmer, but leaving doubts about his supremacy over the former titlist. Those doubts were erased in August of the same year, when Tiger stopped Fullmer, who surrendered after six bloody, one-sided rounds in Ibadan. (It was the last bout of Fullmer's career.) The victory further boosted Tiger's status as a national hero.

"It was pandemonium that night at Liberty Stadium, Ibadan," noted Lloyd Garrison, writing some years later in The New York Times. "Everyone who counted [in the country] was at ringside." Among those in attendance was the country's ceremonial president, Dr. Nnamdi Azikiwe. The fight was arranged by Jack Solomons, the legendary British promoter of the '50s and '60s.

Contacted by THE RING, Fullmer said, "If I was gonna lose to somebody, I can't think of anyone I would rather have lost to than Tiger. He was a very courageous fighter, and as cordial a man as anyone I've ever met. When I fought him in Nigeria, he was gracious, and I was treated as well as anywhere else I ever fought—and maybe better.

"Whenever I'm asked about the best fighters I ever faced, I always put Tiger right up there."

To cap Tiger's achievements, and in recognition of his international popularity, the British government awarded him membership in the Order of the British Empire (OBE). However, in December '63, only four months after his win over Fullmer in Ibadan, Tiger lost the title to Giardello in Atlantic City. Paul Cavalier, the referee and sole judge, ruled in favor of the more fleet-footed and sharpshooting challenger.

Over the next 22 months, Tiger, hoping to secure a return vs. Giardello, had to reestablish himself against the leading contenders of the day. In October 1964, he knocked out Jose Gonzalez. In March 1965, he stopped roly poly Argentine Rocky Rivero. And two months later, he scored three knockdowns en route to a decision victory over the highly rated Hurricane Carter. All three bouts were held at Madison Square Garden.

Tiger was rewarded with another title

Appendix 1

shot, and he reclaimed the world title from Giardello in October 1965. This time, his heavier punching secured a points victory.

Asked to recall his memories of his rival, Giardello told THE RING, "He was one of the best. I know because I fought him four times. I was one of the first guys he fought when he came over from England [in 1959]. I didn't think much of him. I didn't really train that hard, and he beat me. He was a very strong guy. And a gentleman. One thing I always remember about him: If you hit him low, he didn't complain about it like the fighters of today. He was a real professional."

Like Fullmer, Giardello asked, "Has it really been 25 years since his death?"

In April 1966, welterweight champion Emile Griffith outpointed Tiger, stripping him of the middleweight crown. About the same time, the political situation in Nigeria was changing drastically, with developments leading to a bloody three-year civil war that would significantly affect Tiger's life. For although his fighting bases were in Europe and America, Tiger's roots remained firmly planted in his Eastern Nigerian homeland of Aba. He and his wife Abigail had raised a family of eight children, and he had invested considerable portions of his earnings in real estate in the federal capital of Lagos.

The political turmoil in Nigeria had its genesis in a military coup in January 1966, spearheaded by officers of Tiger's tribal group, the Igbos, from the predominantly Christian South Eastern Region. Nigeria's civilian government, which had been inaugurated following the end of British colonial rule in October 1960, was violently overthrown. The prime minister, Sir Tafawa Balewa, and many prominent political figures of Northern Nigerian origin were brutally assassinated. Thus, the hope that Nigeria would emerge as one of the more stable of the world's new nations was shattered. The coup set in motion a chain of domestic violence that in time would escalate into pogroms and massacres, and then into a full-scale civil war.

In July 1966, a counter coup was launched by the Northern elements in a reprisal targeted mainly against the Igbos of the East for the role they had played in the first coup. During the following weeks and months, attacks were made against the tribal group, followed by the destruction and looting of assets and properties of many of its members who had settled outside their home regions. Tiger, formerly a symbol of Nigeria's national pride, technically became a traitor when, in good conscience, he later identified with and elected to fight alongside his Igbo kinsmen.

So charged were the emotions that even three decades after the end of the hostilities, Chief Balogun, who had been a staunch Federalist at the time of the crisis, still finds the fighter's decision abhorrent. "Tiger ruined himself," the Chief stated with indignation when interviewed by THE RING. "He committed treason by joining in the Biafran rebellion, ignoring the counseling we gave him. Had he been wiser and not involved himself in the futile parochial cause, his life story would most certainly have been more glorious."

Before getting caught up in the civil war, Tiger further uplifted his international record by becoming only the second middleweight champion to win the light heavyweight title. (The first was Bob Fitzsimmons.) In December 1966, barely six months after losing the 160-pound crown to Griffith, Tiger, 37, dethroned 175-pound world champion Jose Torres at Madison Square Garden. A 3-1 underdog, Tiger spotted the champion eight pounds and, over the course of 15 rounds, fought far more aggressively, winning by unanimous decision.

Back in Tiger's homeland, the civil crisis had by then escalated into full-blown warfare. It was to last from 1967 to 1970. Following unabated attacks on Tiger's Igbo kinsmen in areas outside their domain, a mass exodus of the tribe began, with hundreds of thousands of its nine million members fleeing back to their home region in the east.

In May 1967, the Eastern Nigerian Military Government declared secession from the Nigerian Federation and proclaimed the region the independent republic of Biafra. In the same month that Tiger retained the world light heavyweight title with a split 15-round decision over Torres, he was faced with the option of joining his rebel tribesmen and becoming an enemy of the Nigerian Federation or pledging solidarity with the government and turning his back on his people.

Tiger could have just as easily stood aside and pleaded neutrality or ignored the crisis while safely sojourning abroad. However, as more and more massacres of Igbos flared up in various parts of the North and South Western parts of the country, his conscience beckoned him to take a stand and be counted among his kith and kin. He witnessed first-hand the physical destruction and carnage wreaked on Owerri, one of the several towns and villages of his home region where bombs were dropped indiscriminately by Nigerian Air Force fighter planes. Tiger therefore considered it only honorable to enlist in the Biafran army and join his tribesmen in their struggle for what they considered their collective survival. Like a true patriot, he put his people first, above his self-interest.

Meanwhile, Tiger would make one more successful defense of the light heavyweight title, stopping Roger Rouse in the 12th round in Las Vegas. The bout came in November 1967. Two months later, he announced his having enlisted in the Biafran army to the world press. He proudly displayed his olive green military uniform with its lieutenant's markings and ris-

DICK TIGER

ing sun shoulder band to The *New York Times'* Garrison, who visited him in the Biafran stronghold of Port Harcourt. Asked why he had joined the army, Tiger responded, "I've never been afraid to fight in the ring, and I'm not afraid to fight for my country."

Despite the obvious fact that he need not see actual combat and could serve well as a morale booster for the Biafran troops and an international public relations functionary for their cause, he expressed his readiness to go to the front if needed.

In May 1968, the 39-year-old Tiger, scaling only 168 pounds, defended the light heavyweight title against the 29-year-old, 6'3" Bob Foster, who enjoyed a 7½-inch advantage in reach. A 12-5 underdog, Tiger acquitted himself creditably in the first round. In the second and third, Foster bombarded the champion with jarring jabs. In the fourth, a chopping hook landed flush on Tiger's chin, and a vicious right uppercut followed. Tiger went down and was counted out. It was the only kayo loss of his 18-year, 84-bout career. As humble in defeat as he had always been in victory, he praised and credited Foster, then vowed to fight on.

As the Nigerian civil war raged on from 1968 through '69, Tiger shuttled between his war-torn homeland and the Western world, flying circuitous air routes to evade the Nigerian authorities while plying his trade. Though he would never again engage in a world title fight, he still had a number of major victories to score.

In October 1968, five months after losing the title to Foster, Tiger and Frankie DePaula duked it out in a wild and savage battle in New York City. The fighters each scored two knockdowns in the first four rounds before Tiger roared ahead and ultimately outpointed his opponent over 10 rounds. The action-packed duel was designated Fight of the Year by THE RING.

In May 1969, Tiger decisioned world middleweight champion Nino Benvenuti in a non-title bout. And six months after that, the 40-year-old former champion gained recognition as number-one challenger by outscoring Andy Kendall.

It was also in 1969 that in protest against British military support of Nigeria in the ongoing war, Tiger returned the OBE award to the British embassy in Washington, D.C. Writing in December 1971, Phil Pepe of the New York *Daily News* quoted Tiger's rationale. He couldn't keep the medal, Tiger had said, "because every time I look at it, I think of the millions of men, women, and children who are dying" in the Nigerian-Biafran war.

Tiger, Africa's first multiple world champion, had his last fight in July 1970, a month short of his 41st birthday. He lost on points to Griffith. By this time the civil war had ended, with the secessionist Biafrans having been completely overrun by the Nigerian Federal forces. During the war, Tiger had remained loyal to the cause of his kinsmen, and as the rebel leaders capitulated, he faced the reality of the situation without remorse or bitterness. His real estate investments in Lagos, estimated by him at $103,000, had either been requisitioned or confiscated by the federal authorities. Yet, as Tiger told the *New York Times* just before the second Griffith fight, "Now it's all Nigeria again. Now that the war is over, I am from Nigeria again. After this fight, I hope to go home again to see my family."

After the loss to Griffith, Tiger chose not to be relegated to trialhorse status. He announced his retirement in early-1971. His final record: 61-17-3 (26). Desperate for income, he worked briefly as a security guard at the Metropolitan Museum of Art in New York City. Having worked as a watchman in the early-'50s, he had traveled full-circle.

In July 1971, Tiger was hospitalized in New York, during which doctors diagnosed cancer of the liver. The man who had refused to forsake his people in their time of need decided to return home to die among them. On December 14, 1971, Tiger, 42, a three-time world champion, died in Aba, near his birthplace of Amaigbo, Orlu. He was virtually penniless, but he passed in the arms of family and loved ones.

After Tiger's death, Jersey Jones, his American manager, estimated that the champion had earned about half-a-million dollars during his 18-year ring career. This was by no means a meager sum by the standards of the day, and it rated as a most handsome, if not stupendous, fortune in Tiger's homeland, where the economy receded severely in the decades following his death. All of Tiger's money was lost during the war. But he never complained, citing that he wasn't the only one who had lost everything.

Tiger's legacy was much more than his fighting record, which remains unsurpassed by any other African pugilist a quarter-century after his retirement. He was able to ensure the education of his children, one of whom is presently a practicing lawyer in Nigeria. Throughout his fighting prime, he sent money and gifts home to his family, and even as his earnings grew, he was known to have lived very frugally abroad.

After Tiger's death, the tributes from the boxing community flowed. Teddy Brenner, then the matchmaker at Madison Square Garden, said, "Tiger could have held his own with any [fighter] in any era, the Robinsons, the LaMottas, the Grebs, and the Mickey Walkers." In the encyclopedic *Pictorial History Of Boxing*, THE RING publisher and editor Nat Fleischer described Tiger as "one of boxing's best-liked heroes." He was portrayed as "sincere, modest, affable, and gentlemanly ... a man of conscience."

Even Chief Balogun, who had grave misgivings over the fighter's insistence on joining in the ill-fated Biafran campaign, and who severed all relations with Tiger following that decision, expresses nothing but respect. "No matter our differences," he said, "I will always fly the Tiger's kite. He was a truly great fighter and a good and selfless man. His memory is one I will cherish until the day I die."

Tiger continues to rank highly in a professional sense as well. In rating the 40 middleweight titlists between 1884 and 1980, THE RING placed Tiger sixth, behind only Sugar Ray Robinson, Carlos Monzon, Stanley Ketchel, Griffith, and Harry Greb. He was twice named Fighter of the Year by both the Boxing Writers Association and THE RING, and in the April 1996 issue of this magazine, he was placed first on an all-time top-10 list of African fighters.

Boxing will never forget Dick Tiger. What is left to be done is for the Nigerian government to rehabilitate his image by establishing in his homeland an enduring and befitting monument to his memory. The Nigerian civil war is long over. In completing the healing process of the wounds suffered by millions of innocent souls, Tiger ought to be paid the final dues that he so richly deserves. ■

Adedamola Ifaturoti, who, like Tiger, is a Nigerian, is The Ring's correspondent for Africa.

APPENDIX 2

Review of the Original Edition of the Tiger biography by *The Ring* Magazine in its July 2002 issue

THE BOXING BOOKSHELF

Although former middleweight and light heavyweight champion Dick Tiger is the most famous African fighter of all-time, most school children (and many adults) in his native Nigeria have never even heard of him. This sad state of affairs could be rectified by the recent publication of *Dick Tiger: The Life & Times Of Africa's Most Accomplished World Boxing Champion* (Sungai Books, 110 pages, paperback) by Damola Ifaturoti.

The author, who emigrated from Nigeria to the United States in 1998, embarked on this labor of love in the hopes of restoring Tiger to his rightful status as a true hero.

"I would like to educate young Nigerians about Tiger's accomplishments and exemplary life," said Ifaturoti. "I also wanted to settle the issue of his involvement in the Biafran war."

It was Tiger's role in the 1967 Nigerian civil war that led to his neglected status at home and also provides material for the most riveting chapter in Ifaturoti's book. Unfortunately for Tiger, he was on the losing side, and when the separatist movement was crushed in '70, he lost most of his assets and fell into disfavor with the ruling establishment.

An indication of how deep Nigeria's ethnic rivalries still run is that some factions were surprised that Ifaturoti, a member of the Yoruba clan, was writing a book about Tiger, an Igbo. But the fact that Ifaturoti's book was launched at a luncheon at Nigeria House in New York City, with both Nigeria's United Nations representative and Consol General on hand for the proceedings, indicated that the official attitude toward Tiger, who died of cancer in '71, has softened.

Ifaturoti feels that recognizing Tiger's deeds as an athlete and his nobility as a man could work as a unifying force for all Nigeria, a nation still racked by political instability and ethnic rivalries.

Copies of *Dick Tiger* can be purchased for $18 each (postage included) by writing to: Damola Ifaturoti, 14-08 Deer Creek Drive, Plainsboro, NJ 08536.

—**Nigel Collins**

APPENDIX 3

Author's article "The Best of a Nation: The All Time Top Ten of Africa" published in *The Ring* Magazine April 1996 issue

Appendix 3

England, turning pro at flyweight and growing into a workmanlike featherweight. He won the vacant world title by rising from the canvas to shoot down the favored Cherif Hamia (KO 10) in 1957. He made one defense before being dethroned by Davey Moore. His victims included Miguel Berrios, Jean Sneyers, and a faded Willie Pep. Career record: 59-13-2 (21).

•**Ayub Kalule** was a clever southpaw from Uganda who, while no kayo puncher, was far stronger than most of his opponents. Fighting out of Denmark, he won the British Commonwealth middleweight title, then dropped down to junior middleweight and captured WBA honors by outpointing Masashi Kudo in 1979. He made four defenses before being dethroned by Sugar Ray Leonard (KO by 9) in '81. He was good enough to win the European middleweight title in 1985, and long after his prime. Career record: 46-4 (23).

•**Sumbu Kalambay** is the best fighter ever produced by Zaire. Based in Italy, he was a quick middleweight who was skilled enough to issue Mike McCallum his first loss in 33 bouts. He won the vacant WBA title by scoring a points victory over Iran Barkley in 1987, and followed with defenses against McCallum (W 12), Robbie Sims (W 12), and Doug DeWitt (KO 7). In a shocker, he was dethroned by the featherfisted Michael Nunn via one-punch, first-round kayo. Record: 57-6-1 (32).

•**Cornelius Boza-Edwards** was among the most exciting TV performers of the early-'80s, when the junior lightweight division featured fight of the year candidates in nearly every title bout. The Ugandan-born, England-based southpaw was a classic boxer who invariably brawled. He won the WBC title by decisioning Bazooka Limon in 1981, and successfully defended against Bobby Chacon (KO 13). Other victims included John Verderosa, Robert Elizondo, Choo Choo Brown, Melvin Paul, and John Montes. Career record: 45-7-1 (34).

•**Ike Quartey** is the reigning WBA welterweight champion. The potential of the Ghanaian seems limitless, and a unification victory over WBC titlist Pernell Whitaker would seal his greatness. A terrific puncher, Quartey, 25, won the African junior welter title in only his 12th pro bout. He captured the WBA 147-

Nigeria's Hogan Bassey moves inside against Carmelo Costa

pound crown by stopping the previously unbeaten Crisanto Espana (KO 11) in 1994, and has made three defenses. Career record: 30-0 (26).

•**John Mugabi** used to say in his limited English, "I will knock him out." It was fitting, as the Ugandan-born slugger, a silver medalist at the 1980 Olympics, scored kayos in all of his pro wins. He ran into Marvin Hagler (KO by 11) in his first title shot, but succeeded in his third try, crushing Rene Jacquot (KO 1) for the WBC 154-pound crown in 1989. He beat, among others, Frank Fletcher, Curtis Parker, Earl Hargrove, and Hard Rock Green, but also suffered first-round kayo defeats at the hands of Terry Norris and Gerald McClellan. Career record: 38-4 (38).

•**David Kotey**, nicknamed "Poison," won the featherweight title of Africa, the British Commonwealth title, and, in 1975, the WBC title, surprising Ruben Olivares on points. The Ghanaian made two defenses before losing a decision to Danny Lopez in Accra. In an international sense, his time at the top was brief, but his victory over the legendary Olivares merits a spot in the top 10. Career record: 38-6-1 (23). ∎

Adedamola A. Ifaturoti, who is based in Ibadan, Nigeria, is a correspondent for The Ring.

Ghana's Azumah Nelson lands low vs. Mario Martinez

Uganda's Corny Boza-Edwards connects vs. Bobby Chacon

BIBLIOGRAPHY

Books

Andre, Sam, and Nat Fleischer. *A Pictorial History of Boxing: From the Bare-knuckled Days to the Present.* New York: Carol Publishing Group, 1989.

Benson, Peter. *Battling Siki: A Tale of Ring Fixes, Race, and Murder in the 1920s:* Fayetteville: The University of Arkansas Press, 2006.

Collins, Nigel. *Boxing Babylon: Behind the Shadowy World of the Prize Ring:* New York: Carol Publishing Group, 1990.

Fleischer, Nat, Bert Sugar and Herbert G. Goldman et al., eds. *The Ring Record Book & Boxing Encyclopedia 46 Vols. 1941 - 1967*: New York: Ring Bookshop and others,

Mullan, Harry. *The Great Book of Boxing:* New York: Crescent Books, 1987.

Mullan, Harry. *The Illustrated History of Boxing:* New York Crescent Books, 1987.

Roberts, James B. and Alexander G. Skutt. *The Boxing Register; International Boxing Hall of Fame Official Record Book 2nd Edition.* McBooks Press, Ithaca, New York, 1998

Bibliography

Weston, Stanley, and Steven Farhood. *The Ring:* Chronicling of Boxing. London: Hamlyn, 1993

Journals, Magazines & Other Periodicals
- *Boxing 98* (and prior years)
- *The Boxing Record Book*, Fight Fax, Inc
- *Boxing News*
- *International Boxing Digest*
- *K.O.*
- *The New York Times*
- *The Ring* The Bible of Boxing
- *The New York Daily News*
- *Sports Illustrated*

Websites

- Home page of Uzoma Onyemaechi
  http://www-personal.si.umich.edu/~uzo/HomePage.html
- World of Boxing
  http://www.boxing.clara.net/
- International Boxing Hall of Fame
  http://www.ibhof.com/
- Internet Boxing Records Archives
  http://www2.xtdl.com/~brasslet//index.html
- The World Boxing Association (WBA)
  http://www.wbaonline.com/
- Boxing Times
  http://www.boxingtimes.com/

ABOUT THE AUTHOR

'Damola Ifaturoti was born in Lagos, Nigeria and had his secondary education at Government College Ibadan. He holds a bachelor's degree in Political Science from the University of Ife (now Obafemi Awolowo University), Ile-Ife Nigeria. He has also undergone various training programs in his professional field of book publishing over the years, including the 2001 World Bank Workshop on Information Technology and Publishing. He has also completed continuing studies programs in Computer Networking and Web Development at Indiana University, Indianapolis, and the Princeton Adult School, Princeton, New Jersey respectively.

'Damola worked with Evans Publishers, a leading book publishing house in Nigeria for over a decade, serving in various editorial and administrative positions from 1987 till 1998 when he resigned as Deputy Controller, Admin Services to relocate to the United States with his family. He was for a number of years in the 1990s, a member of the editorial board and later Editor-in-Chief of *The Publisher*, official journal of the Nigerian Publishers Association (NPA). Between 1999 and 2015 he served as Senior Editor and Editorial Coordinator with Africa World Press, Trenton, New Jersey. He presently runs AMV Publishing Services LLC - an independent small press based out of Princeton Junction, New Jersey.

About the Author

'Damola has been an avid writer whose works have spanned a wide range of themes and subjects. They include commentary on various contemporary political issues, essays on corporate and professional topics relating to the book publishing industry in Africa and articles on popular international sporting figures and events. His articles have been published in national, regional, and international periodicals and publications including the now defunct *Daily Sketch* newspapers of Nigeria, *The African Publishing Review:* official organ of the African Publishers Network (APNET), Harare Zimbabwe, *The Bellagio Publishing Network Newsletter,* Oxford UK and *The Ring* Magazine: *The Bible of Boxing,* U.S.A.

'Damola presently lives with his family in Princeton Junction, New Jersey and has a home base in his birthplace of Lagos, Nigeria.

The Author with Editor of *The Ring* Magazine, Nigel Collins at a presentation ceremony of the original edition of the biography at the Nigerian Consulate in Manhattan New York, 2002.

The Author at a promotional event in New York in 2003 flanked by two of Dick Tiger's championship fight opponents — Jose Torres of Puerto Rico (World Light Heavyweight Champion) and Emile Griffith of the Virgin Islands (World Middleweight Champion).

The Author with Dick Tiger's widow, Mrs. Abigail Ihetu and daughter, Ms. Justina Ihetu at the conclusion of an arranged meeting interview session at Justina's home in the Bronx, New York in 2001

INDEX

A

Adebo, Simeon, 51
Adinoyi-Ojo, Onukaba, xi,
Aguiyi-Ironsi, Major General Johnson, 57, 105
Ali, Muhammad, 78, 91
Ama, John, xxix, 6
Amaigbo, xvi, xxv, xxviii, xxix, 1, 4, 5, 12, 19, 61, 64, 79, 82, 86, 89, 90
Anderson, Dave, 83
Archer, Joey, xxi, 23
Armstrong, Gene, xxx, 13, 14, 16
Armstrong, Willie, xxx, 10
Azikiwe, Nnamdi, 21

B

Balewa, Sir Abubakar Tafawa, 65-66
Balogun, Chief Ganiyu Kolawole, xii, 3, 73, 87
Bassey, Hogan "Kid", xxiii, 19
Bello, Sir Ahmadu, 66
Benencko, Peter, 6
Benvenuti, Nino, xxvii, xxxi, 78
Biafra, xxiv, xxvii, 71,75,81

Boxing Register, Official Record Book of the International Boxing Hall of Fame (IBHOF), The xxxii
Boxing Writers Association of America (BWAA), xxvi, 20, 30, 63
BWAA 1966 Fighter of the Year, 63
BoxRec, xxxii, 4, 5
Boza-Edwards, Cornelius, xxiii,
Brenner, Teddy, 86
British Boxing Board of Control (BBBC), The 21
British Empire (Commonwealth) Middleweight Title, xxv, xxxii, 11, 25

C

Calhoun, Rory, xxx, 13, 47
Canastota, xxviii, 88
Candlestick Park, San Francisco, 19, 29
Carpentier, Georges, xxiii,
Carter, Rubin "Hurricane", xxxi, 23-24, 38
Casey, Hank, xxx, 16
Cavalier, Paul, 22

Cerdan, Marcel, 88
Citro, Ralph, 12, 32
Collins, Nigel, vi, x

D

Daily Times of Nigeria, xi, 33-35, 39-41, 47, 49-52, 54, 61, 62
Dean, Alan, xxix, xxx, 7, 8, 9, 10
Delargy, Paddy, xxx, 10
DePaula, Frank, xxvii, xxxi, 44, 77-78 Dori, Marius, xxx, 9
Downes, Terry, xxx, 9
Dynamite, Easy, xxix, 4

E

Early Professional Career, 1-6
Eastern Region, Nigeria, xxiv, xxvii, 3.49, 64, 66-71
Edwards, Phil, xxx, 10
Ellaway, Billy, xxx, 11
Eme, Simon, xxix, 4
European Boxing Union (EBU), 21

F

Fagbemi, Roy, xxix, 5
Fajuyi, Adekunle, 68
Fall, Amadou Louis M'Barick (also see Battling Siki), xxiii
Farhood, Steve, xii
Farnsworth, Jack, 6
Fernandez, Florentino, xxx, 17-18
Fitzsimmons, Bob, 21

Fleischer, Nat, xx, 39, 87
Foster, Bob, xxi, xxvii, xxxi, 56, 75, 79
Fullmer, Don, xxxi, 23
Fullmer, Gene, xii, xx, xxvi, xxx, xxxi, 17, 19, 26, 27-29, 87, 90

G

Garrison, Lloyd, xii, 20, 74
Gerhadt, David M., xx
Giardello, Joey, xii, xx, xxvi. xxx, xxxi, 13, 22, 30, 32, 42, 59, 63
Gonzalez, Jose, xxi, 23
Gowon, Colonel Yakubu, xxvii, 69
Greaves, Wilf, xxv, xxx, 15
Greb, Harry, 86, 88
Griffith, Emile, xx, xxvi, xxvii, xxxi, 65, 78, 88, 104

H

Hagler, Marvin, 88
Hank, Henry, xxx, 18
Hopkins, Bernard, 88

I

Igbo People/kinsmen, v, xxvii, 1, 2, 21, 49, 64, 65, 66, 67, 68, 69, 70, 72, 74, 80
Ihetu, Abigail, xiv, 12, 33, 34, 35, 48, 50, 62, 64, 77, 82, 87, 104

Index

Ihetu, Charles, 85
Ihetu, Justina, xiv, xv, 85, 87, 104
Ihetu, Richard, v, ix, xvi, xix, xxv, xxxiv, 1, 3, 7, 9, 57, 82, 90, 91,
Ihetu, Richard, Jr., 85
Ihetu, Ubuagwu, 1
International Boxing Hall of Fame (IBHOF), The, xxviii, xxxii, xxxiii, 6, 88, 101,

J

Joe, Mighty, xxix, 4
Johnson, Bolaji, xxix, 5
Johnson, Chief J. M., 27, 39
Jones, Willis "Jersey", 13, 83

K

Kalambay, Sumbu, xxiii
Kalule, Ayub, xxiii
Kendall, Andy, xxxi, 79
Keshi, Ambassador Joe, 91
Ketchel, Stanley, 88
Kid, Koko, xxix, 5
Kotey, David, xxiii

L

Lamotta, Jake, 86
Liberty Stadium Ibadan, 27
Louis, Joe, 36, 42
Lynas, Jimmy, xxix, xxx, 8, 10

M

Madison Square Garden, xx, xxvii, 23, 38, 63, 66, 69, 77-79, 86
Markson, Harry, 86
Mbadiwe, K.O., 49
McAteer, Pat, xxv, xxx, 10
McNally, Gerry, xxix, 8
Mendoza, Gilberto DeJesus, xi
Mendoza, Gilberto, Jr., xi
Merchant, Larry, 82
Mims, Holly, xxx
Monzon, Carlos, 88
Moore, Davey, 30
Mueller, Peter, xxxi, 65
Mugabi, John "The Beast", xxiii

N

National Boxing Association (NBA), The, xx, xxi, xxvi, 11, 21
Nelson, Azumah, xxii, 88
New York Daily News, 79
New York State Athletic Commission (NYAC), The, xxi, 21
New York Times, 20, 74, 80, 83
Niger Delta, 2
Nigerian Boxing Board of Control (NBBC), The, 6
Nigerian Civil War, ix, xxvii, 49, 63, 64, 67, 77-79, 84, 87, 89

Nigerian Military coup of January 1966, 65-67
Nigerian Military counter coup of July 1966, 67
Nuanne, Robert, xxix, 5
Nzeogwu, Major Chukwuma Kaduna, 65

O

Odumegwu-Ojukwu, Colonel Chukwuemeka, xxvii, 69, 70, 80
Ogbuji, Abigail, 12
Okpara, Peter, xxix, 5
Onyemaechi, Uzoma, 2

P

Pepe, Phil, xii, 79
Pickett, Bill, xxx, 16
Pictorial History of Boxing, The, 87
Poison, Jean, xxx, 10
Pompey, Yolande, xxx, 11
Power, Black, xxix, 4
Power, Superhuman, xxix, 5

Q

Quartey, Ike, xxiii

R

Ramos, Sugar, 30
Read, Johnny, xxx, 11
Ring Magazine, The vi, ix, xxii, xxvi, xxvii, xxviii, 14, 20 39, 44, 63, 73, 74, 76, 78, 87, 88, 92, 97, 98
Ring Magazine 1962 Fighter of the Year, xxvi, 20
Ring Magazine 1965 Fighter of the Year, xxvi, 63
Ring Magazine 1967 Round of the Year,
Ring Magazine 1968 Round of the Year, xxvii
Rivero, Rocky "Roly Poly", xxxi, 23
Robinson, Sugar Ray, 24, 86, 88
Roe, George, xxix, 8
Rose, Lion, xxix, 4
Rouse, Roger, xxvii, xxxi, 74
Rowley, Dennis, xxix, 8
Ruellet, Jean, xxx, 10

S

Sandy, Randy, xxx, 12
Scott, Wally, xxix, 8
Siki, Battling, xxiii, 100
Solomons, Jack, 20, 54

T

Tale of the Tape: Dick Tiger versus Joey Giardello, 32
Tale of the Tape: Gene Fullmer Versus Dick Tiger, 28

Index

Tonica, Abraham, xxxi, 70
Torres, Jose, xxi, xxvi, xxxi, 54, 55, 66, 68, 71, 103

U
Udenwa, Achike, xiv, xvi-xix

W
Walker, Mickey, 86
Webb, Spider, xxx, 11, 16, 45

West, Tommy, xxxix, xxxiii, 4, 5
World Boxing Association (WBA), The, xi, xxi
World Boxing Council (WBC), The, xxii, xxiii

Z
Zalazar, Victor, xxx, 15
Zale, Tony, 24

www.ingramcontent.com/pod-product-compliance
Lightning Source LLC
Chambersburg PA
CBHW020425010526
44118CB00010B/431